The Gasconade Review presents:
Gas Station Famous

Edited by John Dorsey and Jason Ryberg

Spartan Press
Kansas City, MO
spartanpresskc@gmail.com

OAC Books
Belle, MO
www.osageac.org

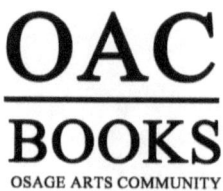
OSAGE ARTS COMMUNITY

Copyright © Jason Ryberg, 2018
First Edition 1 3 5 7 9 10 8 6 4 2
ISBN: 978-1-946642-76-9
LCCN: 2018911903

Design, edits and layout: Jason Ryberg
Title page and exit images: Jon Lee Grafton
All rights reserved. No part of this publication may be reproduced or transmitted in any form or by any means, electronic or mechanical, including photocopying, recording or by info retrieval system, without prior written permission from the author.

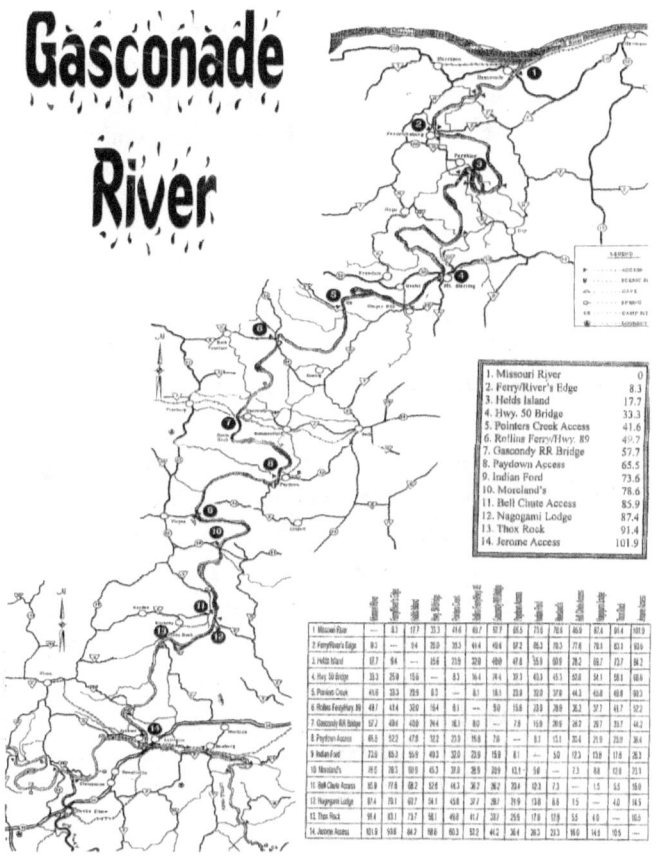

The **Gasconade River** is about 280 miles (450 km) long and is located in central and south-central Missouri in the United States. The Gasconade River begins in the Ozarks southeast of Hartville in Wright County and flows generally north-north-eastwardly through Wright, Laclede, Pulaski, Phelps, Maries, Osage and Gasconade counties, through portions of the Mark Twain National Forest. It flows into the Missouri River near the town of Gasconade in Gasconade County.

The name Gasconade is derived from "Gascon", an inhabitant of the French region of Gascony. The people of that province were noted for their boastfulness. It was applied by the early French to the Indians living on its banks who bragged about their exploits. The name means to boast or brag, and thus the river received its name. The waters of the river are boisterous and boastful and the name is also descriptive.

The headwaters of the Gasconade are in the southeastern corner of Webster County northeast of Seymour, Missouri where it drains the eastern margin of the Springfield Plateau at approximately 37°11'54"N 92°41'44"W. The river joins the Missouri River at the city of Gasconade at 38°40'28"N 91°32'55"W The river follows a meandering course through the Ordovician age dolostone and sandstone bedrock of the Ozark Salem Plateau creating spectacular bluffs and incised meanders along the way. Numerous springs and caves occur within the drainage area and along the river course. Significant tributaries include the Osage Fork of Webster and Laclede counties and Roubidoux Creek and Big Piney River of Texas and Pulaski counties. The Roubidoux and Big Piney flow respectively along the west and east boundaries of Fort Leonard Wood which lies a short distance south and east of the Gasconade.

The plateau surface near the midpoint is 300 feet (91 metres) above the river bottom near the river midpoint northeast of Waynesville creating scenic river bluffs. At the junction with the Missouri the river bottom is about 400 feet (120 m) lower in elevation than the old plateau surface above the river. The elevation of the plateau rim at the headwaters is at or above 1,600 feet (490 m) with local hilltops at over 1,700 feet (520 m) (second highest elevation in Missouri near Cedar Gap). The elevation at the confluence with the Missouri is 500 feet (150 m) giving an overall drainage basin relief of 1,200 feet (370 m).

It is ranked with a difficulty of I and II (seldom) by those who canoe, kayak and float. It is considered a good float stream because there's typically not a heavy congestion of boats. It is common to go for many miles without seeing another boat.

There are caves and an abundance of wildlife along the river and is considered a popular place by anglers for its largemouth bass and smallmouth bass.

The Gasconade River is the longest river completely within the boundary of Missouri. It has been called one of the world's crookedest rivers.

The **Gasconade Review** is a literary and arts publication based out of the Osage Arts Community (http://osageac.org/), located on the Gasconade River, just outside of Belle, Missouri. It appears twice annually, focusing primarily, but not exclusively, on writers and artists from the region and state, but occasionally also features *folks what ain't from around here*. All submissions must be hand delivered between the months of April and October and the hours of 3pm to 6pm. A decent bourbon is appreciated. Proper river attire required. Don't worry, the dogs won't bite.

The Gasconade Review was created as part of Belle's Poet Laureate project at the beginning of 2017. Originally founded as a means to showcase work by poets and artists from around the fine state of Missouri, our scope has since grown to include pieces from all over the American Midwest, and we're darn proud to be able to offer you the works in the volume you're currently holding in your hands.

—John Dorsey, Founding Co-Editor and first Poet Laureate of Belle, 2017-2019

CONTENTS

Pecos Park by Greg Edmondson / 1

Dan Smith

Belief System / 2
Thank You Jim Jarmusch / 5
A Bad Ron Padgett Imitation / 7

Don Kloss

Carnivorous Signals / 9
The Geometry of Agriculture / 11
Indications of Familiarity / 13

Mark Sebastian Jordan

Rust Wars / 15
Pronouncement / 18
Kundalinear / 20

Natural Selection by Greg Edmondson / 21

Jason Baldinger

Beckemeyer Illinois 1958 / 22
A Palomino and a Bull Snake / 24
Postcard from Huron, Indiana / 25

Victor Clevenger

christian ready for the fire / 26
public enemy / 28
a poem written after pulling memoirs of a street
   poet off the shelf on the night that i heard frankie
   died / 29

Agnes Vojta

December / 30
the spring rains were relentless / 31
Luxury / 32

Recombinant by Greg Edmondson / 33

April Pameticky

True Story / 34
Goldfish / 36
Hair / 37

K.W. Peery

Room in the Trunk / 39
Night Train / 41
Claw Hammer Headache / 43

James Benger

Drip / 44
Infinite / 45
Red / 46

The Druid by Karl Ramberg / 47

Dan Wright

Omit the Logic / 48
House Show / 51
Viva la Revolution? / 53

Nathanael William Stolte

Grey Brother / 54
July Valentine / 57
Friday the 13th, October. 2006 / 59

Scot Young

down a redneck dirt road / 61
white rabbits / 63
I-435 & Truman Road / 65

Lamp of Life by Karl Ramberg / 67

Zach Fishel

Every Reason / No Reason / 68
Walking at Sunset Crater, as your Wife Laughs
   at the Word Volcano / 69
Habit / 70

Jason Mayer

A Trip Home / 71

Dianne Borsenik

Finding Myself Inside a Quentin Tarantino Movie
   in Cleveland at Four O'clock in the Afternoon / 98
Seeing Jim Morrison in Giant Eagle
   on the First Day of Autumn / 99
This Can't Be Oklahoma / 101

The Cedar by Karl Ramberg / 102

Jeanette Powers

The Creek Calls the Storm Waters / 103

Steve Brightman

Aphrodite Put Her Faith in the Golden Apple
   to Distract Her from a Corrugated Heart / 108
Dionysus Abandons His Children at the First
   Promise of Skin Falling Upon Other Skin / 109
The Face of the Closest Woman to Zeus is the
   Face of Every Woman to Zeus / 110

John Clayton

Good Luck Bad Luck / 111
My Sister / 113
The Box / 115

Bottle on Fence Post by John E. Epic / 117

Michael Joseph Arcangelini

Sleeping with Fireflies / 118
A Slow Collapse / 120
Marcus Considers a Dog / 122

Hunter Pender

This is one of many times I have written
   about you / 124
I am sitting alone with a cold cup of coffee / 126
Dreams of cemented skies / 128

Jane McElroy Butler

Autumnal Devotions / 130
Searching / 131
The Storm / 133

Tractors and Chevy by John E. Epic / 134

Michael Hackney

Amazing & Delicious / 135
Cincinnati / 136
The Problem / 137

Kerry Trautman

The Sound of Your Own Voice / 138
Wisdom / 140
Roasting Turkey for Friends / 143

Daniel Crocker

How Me and Lord Byron Got our Grooves Back / 144
C is for Cookie / 147
Mania Makes Me A Better Poet / 149

Portrait of Jason Ware by John E. Epic / 153

Paul Koniecki

Because It Has
  No Natural Enemies / 154
The Dells - July 1976 / 156
Too Late to Miss the Brewery Work / 158

RC Patterson

What Does It Mean to be a Realist? / 159
Elegy 1 of Erotica Matrix / 160
Trapped Like Mice / 161

John Dorsey

Passing Through Leadwood / 162
Rosalea Ain't Dead Yet / 164
A Ghost is an Unforgiving River / 166

Harmonize by Joel Lipman / 167

Jackie Magnuson Ash

Season's End / 168
Makeshift / 169
First Fall / 170

John Macker

Border Wall Blues / 171
Empty Foxhole / 174
Buried Poem / 175

Maryfrances Wagner

The Immigrants Get a New Camera / 177
Demoni / 178
Zia Rosie Talks About the Family Farm / 180

The Brain by Joel Lipman / 182

Xanath Caraza

El huracán / 183
  The Hurricane / 184
El mar se vuelve espejo / 185
  The Sea Turns Mirror / 186
Oleaje / 187
  Waves / 188

George Wallace

How It Will End / 189
Dream Child Illuminates Herself / 191
Watch Me Burn It To The Ground In The
  Tallgrass, Baby / 192

Chigger Matthews

(for people who laugh at death) /194
bucketshovels at sundown
  (or, where Murphy lay) / 195
To Ronnie with Love / 197

Origins of Poetry: Lines by Joel Lipman / 198

The Players / 199

Gas Station Cashier:

Y'all famous?

Poet:

Only in gas stations.

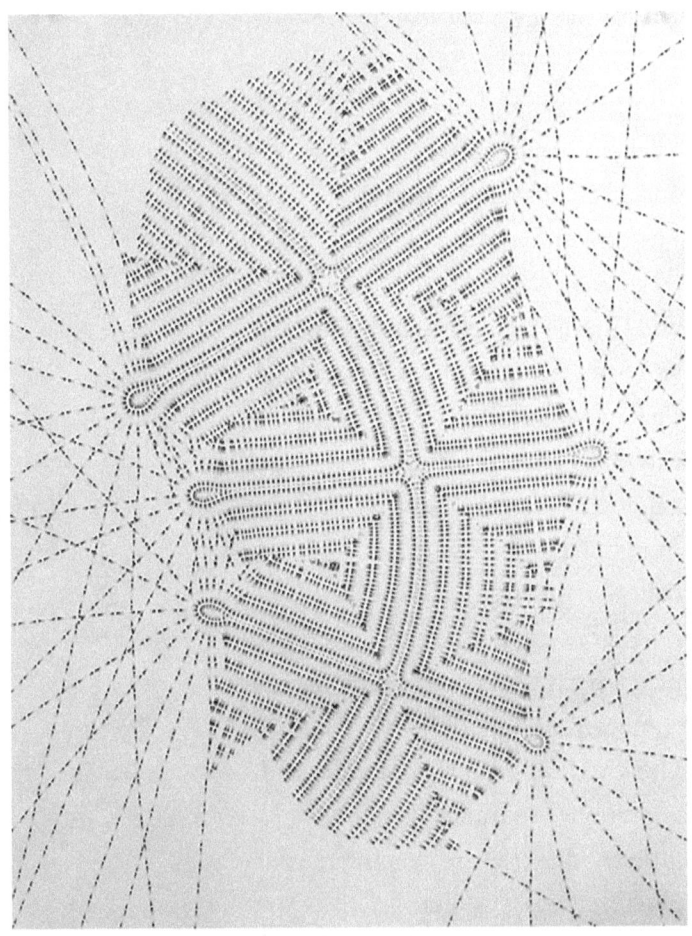

Pecos Park, pencil on paper, 30" x 22", 2010 by Greg Edmondson

Dan Smith

Belief System

I believe in southern rock
and in an alternate universe
I just might be an unmusical
Allman brother
and Charlie Daniels beat the devil
and Sea-Level is highly underrated.
I believe Iris Dement
can make grown men cry
singing *Happy Birthday*
I might have passed
college remedial algebra
if the grad student teacher
hadn't been such an anti-establishment
comedian
I believe Alan Freed was a radio god
and the sweet strange things
little children say are keeping me alive
I believe the sky is blue
due to clinical depression
the ruling class
believes in bread and circuses
anarchists believe in bread
as in a living wage
music is a living breathing thing

not a digital robotic formulaic
assembly line product
live or analog *si*
digital *no*
I believe this is a poem
I believe everyone
is entitled to their beliefs
when I workshop this poem
they will say they want more
I want more
I want movies with plots
and good character development
with fewer special effects
I believe in the comedy
of Ernie Anderson and Tim Conway
I believe our copper river
will turn blue someday
and there should be statues
of comedians not generals
I believe in rock n roll oh did I
say that already I hate when that happens
I believe in my little brother or sister
whom I devoured in utero
I like the idea of San Francisco in the 50's
just the idea never been boy oh man
Dexter and Wardell Anita O what a Day
women in hats and the elegance
of long white gloves

I believe in the deep poetry of Cleveland
like an ore boat pumping bilge
out of rust streaked holes
and deckhands speaking in tongues
to the moonlight rippling in oily water
the bow tenderly French kissing
and the river giving head with old men
fishing off the break wall in the rain
I dream I am a bridge master
opening up for the ore boats
their lights like little jewels in the fog
I dream of her pendulous breasts
blue veined like highways on maps
smoothed out to find lost cities
with steles that tell of ancient mysteries
I believe in the power of Mahalia Jackson
I want People Who Died played at my funeral
I want just one person to like this poem
and I want to be alive when that happens

Thank You Jim Jarmusch

For giving us Paterson.
Putting the ephemeral on film.
I also liked that one with Johnny Depp
and Gary Farmer who was in Pow-Wow
Highway—

Thank you Paterson, NJ
Thank you William Carlos Williams.
Thanks to all the poets scrolling by
on the credits. Thank you Marvin.
You dog—

There is so much there there
in our own private Patersons
that can sometimes sneak up on you
years after your father died and
knock you down like a punch
from Mike Tyson when you
realize you have been surrounded
by poetry the whole time—

Finding out that you wrote the poem
that the young girl reads to Paterson
just knocked me out. I watched it
again last night and I liked it
even more—

I wrote two poems while watching it
and three right after. Water Falls
alright and so do poems plus I
don't have a dog—

A Bad Ron Padgett Imitation

The constable destroyed the painting,
the butcher the meat. Moths zapping butterflies.
Soft, soft the pollinators! that don't sting or bite.
Oh, odes of rain over all it felt good—

Splat! Splat! Splat!

The tv sizzled into ice cream
sandwiches tooting their baloney
with visions of worried looks.
The sewing machines needling
Love's rose. Red ashtrays white butts
crack of marching license plates—

Horrible metronomes keeping time
in line sound effects on sanity.
Rooftops of continents! Tables of contents.
Galaxy doorways! Assembly line syndrome—

The Colonel of Truth
Is lending ears to the pile
driver of History its genitals
swelling with terrorism.
O, shit has it come to this?

A letter from the Marquis.
Sad *"O's"* of poetry in motion.
The rustle of the herds dress rehearsal
for a bad dream about horses asses
one and all illogical zoos. The white rhinos
listening to Picasso's record player
to be named later—

Later Mister Later.

Don Kloss

Carnivorous Signals

It took me
A week to gain
Correct perspective
Understand the significance—

The howls mean some
Have made a kill
A warm deer carcass
For a family meal

It is a signal to the pack—
They identify the location
As do I
What field or wood lot

I now understand
Their silence
Means they are hunting
Could be anywhere

Awareness of every twig snap
Every crinkle of leaves
Or sound in the creek line
Is important

They could be anywhere—
Uneasiness dictates
Every flashlight sweep
Wide as my fear

The Geometry of Agriculture

This place is a sheet of paper
Sporadic pips from a pencil
The only marks
No busy sentences
No blocks of paragraphs

The scattered points
Farm houses and out buildings
Barns and silos
Some freshly painted white or red
Some left to gray over time

Thin lines connect the dots:
Roads that border fields
Cultivated or left as pastures
For livestock—

Rectangles of freshly
Hydroseeded soybeans
Triangles newly dragged
With tractor and disc harrow
Trapezoidal acres
Rows of sprouted feed corn

Guernseys moan low
In indifference to Leghorns
And rams that bleat
Sporadically in a nearby paddock

Winds sweep across the land
Passes of the spring bow compass
Churn up dust
As raking implements
Create furrows in dry clay

The sheet rests held by clips
On a drafting table
The lamp suspended overhead
Shines hot during work hours
Is off and cool
As tractors and protractors
Lie motionless

Indications of Familiarity

When you can tell
When a field of corn
Was planted by its height

You know there are
More ponds
And steel buildings
Than houses

When you know
What livestock is being
Raised on a farm
By the structures

When you know
A grain drier
From a grain silo

You know
What each of the farm
Implements are used
For and when

When you can tell
Hay from straw
From winter wheat

You can't drive
Past a field
Without looking for deer
Along the hedgerow

When you know
These things
Realize you have been
Here a long time

Mark Sebastian Jordan

Rust Wars

You figured out what was happening,
twelve years old, watching the twin suns
rise over the rusty dust of Mansfield, Ohio.
But everyone else—sand people—were blinded
by a cynical feel-good patriotic acting emperor
and knee-jerk hot-button issues. The raiders,
the financial rapists, flayed your family,
left Westinghouse, Tappan, Ohio Brass,
Armco and GM in smoking ruins.

A Grand Canyon was carved
out of the rust here
in the seventies.
It's dug deeper
ever since.

After thirty years,
word is only now leaking out
to the rest of the galaxy that a home planet
was destroyed one morning, princess.
I don't know why they hear so late.
Shouted, I have, for thirty years,
losing friends to my sharp tongue.
But who can look me in the eye?

And who can say: I was wrong?

Once teaching the masses
was nolled as wasted time,
Darth Trump could distract
the grunts long enough
to sell out a land of labor
to the lowest bidder
in order to turn
a quick buck.

Forget
the New Gilded Age,
the gilt wore off
and we're staring
the black eye sockets
of a New Dark Age.
Kneel now, start piling on
the filth in the fields,
(Help, I'm being repressed!)
the old peasant posture
at the foot of a king once more.
What rough beast slouches
toward Cleveland
to be born?

The dark matter of the universe is greed.

Wall Street is building a Death Star.

I'm going to raise this x-wing fighter
out of the swamp, now, for you.

I hope you well I taught.

Pronouncement

who speaks
who speaks

who speaks
who speaks

who speaks
who speaks

the hollow-cheeked mother of winter
is pulling her gray cloak across the sky
is pulling her white blanket across the ground

who speaks
who speaks

memories of the dead, the ones
who shaped families and lives
and hunted and farmed and worked
still linger in the still air

who speaks
who speaks

coyotes on a distant hill
snarl for scraps of power

until their masters in tall towers
blaze their shock collars

who speaks
who speaks

all the sad madmen rumble their trucks
hulking on the horizon—drill baby drill—
star-n-barring it from the land of kingdom went
to the door of the bulging bank

who speaks
who speaks
who speaks

We speak.

Kundalinear

For Lucas Hargis

To see off the shambling dregs of winter,
       to scare up alien gems of twisted purple and green,
   to paint with the richness of ritual and processional,
      to open sealed doors and chart nameless stars,
    to graft neurons that reach from dirt
        to a broken overcast maul of sky,
     We, the enfablers of the old oak dreams,
        we wind our way to the top of the hill,
    gypsies of the zero-point field,
         wishing worlds into startled shape
      with a star-chirp glitter of bells.

        And when you stand before the rest of us,
  Us sprawled in the dusky hillside grass,
     You turning in wondrous poise to speak,
a low slow meteor whistles through
    your starman sphinx silhouette
and penetrates Orion's belt,

Kundalinear.

    A new moon rises
    in your throat
       &
    you tilt your head
    back to the galactic plane
    and sing the clouds away.

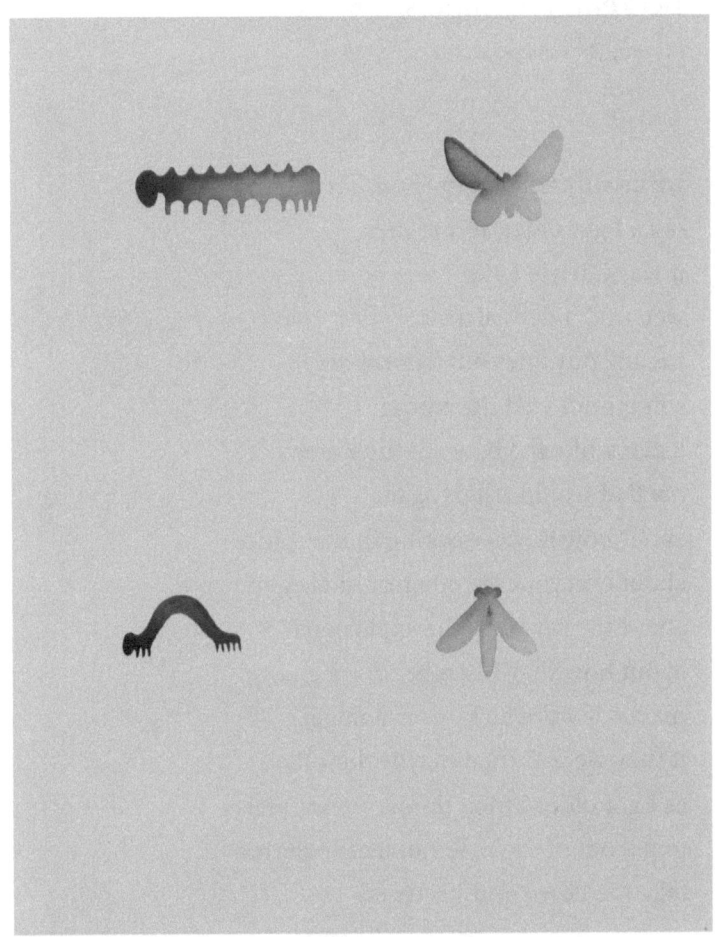

Natural Selection, gouache on paper, 24" x 18", 1996
by Greg Edmondson

Jason Baldinger

Beckemeyer, Illinois 1958
(for Roy Beckemeyer)

we usually headed to Shoal Creek
once I got older, sometimes
it was Carlyle Lake
we'd find a dark alcove
tossing our lines out from shore
sometimes we'd use a boat
listen while the bow cut the water
my dad would tell us again
about how it was working in the mines
about everyone's brother or uncle gone
about the cave-ins, the explosions
about how they lost a hand, a leg
maybe if we're lucky only a finger
if they weren't then maybe their lives
as I got older I took this as a reminder
to get out of town, to not let the mines
take me down and I listened

he would tell us again about our grandfather
a machine runner, how he was running
the air puncher when a ton of slate
came down on him, how it shattered his back
they dug him out and took him to St. Louis

but it was too late, he was gone
no matter how many times he told the story
the hair on my neck always stood up
the helmets we used on these night
we're taken out of the mines
I wondered then if the light
that shown above me
was the last light
my grandfather
had seen

A Palomino and a Bull Snake

there were four water towers on the Salina skyline
more than ten rooms with private baths in the place I stayed
I've lived the last couple days on gin and tequila
there's been no need to hit the brakes over the last eighty miles
it feels like I'm barnstorming a prairie fire

the longest train I ever saw was in Amarillo
that was before today, although it may have been Sheridan
Amarillo is four hundred miles south
Sheridan is a Palomino and a Bull Snake away

in the distance, there's a storm stuck over Topeka
I've seen so much big sky, empty plains
It makes me wanna swing north for the Badlands
I could make Rapid City by morning

yesterday, I learned that Mexican Buffet
are the two most perfect words in the English language
as I left I noticed the only graffiti on the men's room wall
my asshole is burning
except both of the s's were faint, they had been corralled
to some Baptist ranch in the sky, where profanity
is still the devil's tongue

yesterday, I found I can turn bread crumbs into bluebirds
if I head north, gun it to Nebraska
I gonna try my luck turning motels into buffalo

Postcard from Huron, Indiana

I wish you could see
the way the morning
looks dogwood white

trees glow purple
rain soaks
last fall's decay

the road sways
bends between
rock formations
then shoots
down hills
that overlook
hardscrabble
junk farms
mired in mud
newly painted green

Victor Clevenger

christian ready for the fire

with his hair parted
slicked to the right like mine
he orders the kung pow chicken
drizzles sriracha for good measure
then forks a bite

that afternoon at the china restaurant
on old highway 24
i watch my son push through the pain
just to be like his old man

on the drive home
i tell him just wait
because the feeling isn't over

he says   *ugh*
i know
all things that enter
must pass through

you're right   i reassure him

each morning
you'll sit on the cold seat
reflecting on decisions you've made

& some won't feel good
but you'll wipe your ass clean
stand up
wash your hands
look in the mirror
& consider yourself lucky

to still be producing
& breathing the stink

because you're alive
& understand
that the dead

can no longer do
what you
can do

public enemy

if she had a clock
hanging from her neck

rosalea would turn back time

to better days

when the moon
was something lovers
gazed at

from a hotel window

long before the flavor
of the phrase
       fight the power

crossed the cracked
thin skin
of her aging lips

a poem written after pulling *memoirs of a street poet* off the shelf on the night that i heard frankie died

grasping heartbeats
through skin
&
holding firm
like trapping a bee

between cupped hands
& breasts

intrigued

by how it feels

harmless

Agnes Vojta

December

The last days
cling to the year
like late leaves
to the oak trees.

Every song
is a goodbye.

Time's tired steps
echo hollow
in the deserted birds' nests.

the spring rains were relentless

the house struggles
to keep its roof
above water the river
smashes it into trees that
slash the walls
slice the roof
the house thrashes
rips a telephone pole out by its root
crashes
boards swirl
splinters in brown sludge

the round eye
of the satellite dish
does not blink
before drowning

Luxury

I shall splurge
on a box
of black
pencils –
pointy promises that hold
treasures of words.

The rubber end
erases my mistakes,
a luxury
life does not
afford us.

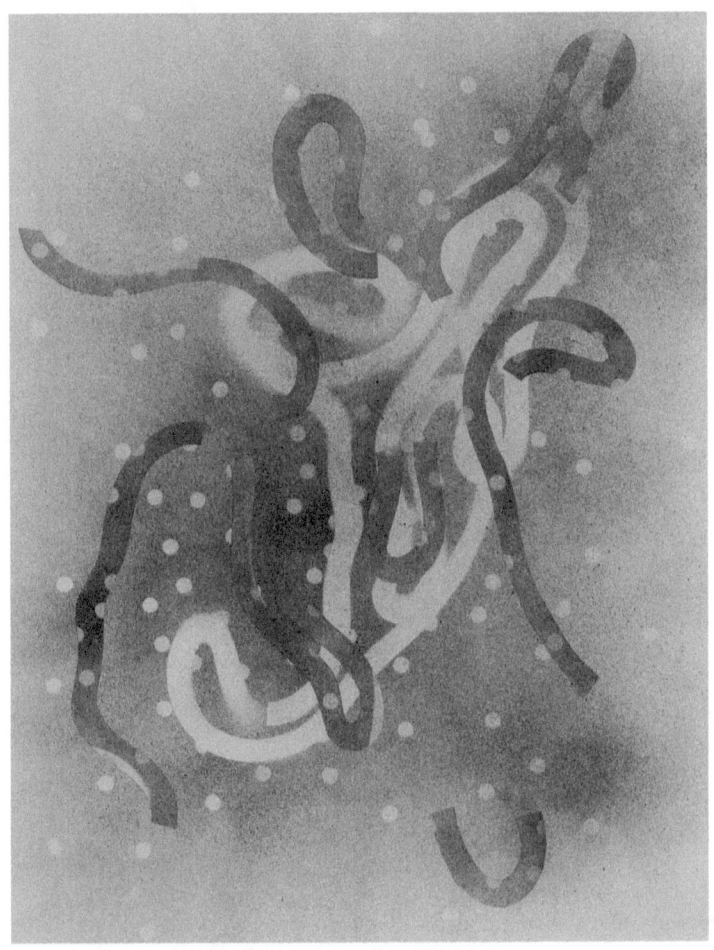

Recombinant, spray paint and collage, 30" x 22", 2014
by Greg Edmondson

April Pameticky

True Story

Remember that time
you took a shit on the restaurant bathroom floor?

Leaving it for the new dish guy you were training,
the one you were supposed to mentor through his broken English.

Do you remember how you told me it was part of his job
       to clean the bathrooms,
          that you even showed him how to add the capful
            of ammonia-rich cleanser in water to mop the floor.

How we hired him so he could send money back to his family,
       hired him instead of your best friend
          that wanted to sell dime bags next to the dish machine.

Do you remember his face when he realized
what was in the corner of men's restroom,

the way he swallowed and closed his eyes to breath
slowly through his open mouth to avoid the smell?

You secretly snickered at him,
       he would never know that you left him a gift.

I heard he bought the restaurant a few years ago,
that his wife changed the menu and runs his kitchen
while his boys run the dish room.

I heard you had to reapply for your job,
    down on your luck,
    presuming on that old relationship
    to pull you from your hole,
    the financial mess you made,
    needing honest work.
You're sober now, working on step 4.

I heard he smiled big at you,
    welcomed you with open arms,
    hugged you as a friend.

I also heard that on your first day back,
he gave you a roll of small doggie bags
    and some rubber dish gloves, just in case
    the bathroom needed cleaning.

Goldfish

Last week I was Fish In Bowl, just me and bubbling pirate's chest.
I could see out, watch television, people playing Yahtzee.

All voices muffled, stretched syllables elongated whale song.
I hunger, wait for pellets to land on surface, to float
   and fly gracefully down.

Last night I was Fish surrounded by green, comforting and warm,
soft curtains that don't scratch what's left of my scales.

Sometimes I am Bird, fly above the surface of the bowl,
sing through air as noise blares and screams,

hurt my brain and my eyes dry from wind,
and so when I break the tension of the water, fall deeper into
   comforting stillness,

I will lie on bottom gravel for a bit, taste each pebble in fracture
   ritual,
list and watch bubbles rise.

Today I swim in circles, tilt and sway. The bottom is up, the top is
   so far away.
I wade through murky water for release, for sustenance, for sound.

Hair

I collect my hairs from shower drains, caught on brass door handles, scraped off
wall pockmarks, car ceilings, desk drawers, the shadow whiskers on his face,
corners where tile meets drywall, endless maws of the vacuum, swirls and mats.

Victorian families collected hair of their dead, twisting strands
onto tangled snarls of curling wire, blooming flowers, growing wreaths
displaying so many shades of keratin brown. Displays would expand
as households would shrink, heirlooms passed from mother to daughter, aunt to heir,
memento mori.

Proper ladies made brooches, corsages, writing letters on their techniques.
Pam and I found a hair museum on a road trip to Independence.
Lost and curious, we twisted our own hair around twitching fingers,
considered the inhuman colors modern dyes allowed modern us.

My children, a genetic lottery, wheat waves, and amber corkscrews,
mixed from the same parental soup, flags shining in the afternoon sun.

Dee insisted that I cut their curls, just a few, she hid them
    away
in a safety deposit box among her opals and jeweled rings,
sealed in plastic bags, air pressed out, where she kept curls
    of her own children.

My husband leaves the white sink powdered in fine, dark
    hairs after a shave,
reminder that I need to clean out the snarls trapped in our
    glass shower.
I drag my index finger, spelling out *Hair* like a child would
    finger
Wash Me on the back of a dirt-encrusted Chevy in a
    Wal-Mart parking lot.

Someday I will wish
I had gathered that dust into bags,
kept it near me in wax and twine,
made a brooch of him,
a final clasp.

K.W. Peery

Room in the Trunk

This
thunder grey
Cadillac
is a
decade
deep
now...

I
paid
a pair
of Russian
brothers...
half what
it was
worth
six years
ago...
at their
buy here
pay here lot
across the
river...

They
claimed
to have
picked
it up
cheap...
at a
police
auction
in East
St. Louis...

And
despite
a few
dents...

it was
cash
well
spent...

With
plenty
of room
in the
trunk
for my
trips to
Texas

Night Train

I
was
sittin'
on
the
couch
in
my
livin'
room...
hangin'
out
with
the
Grateful
Dead...

When
a
stoned
voice
inside
me
said...

*let's
open
another
bottle
of
Night
Train...*

*While
we
wait
for
the
rails
to
fail*

Claw Hammer Headache

This
claw hammer
headache
is unbearable...

So
I drink
and drug
more than
ever before...

Gamblin'
inside
an unknown
diagnosis...

Where
the voices
are deafenin'...

And
Dirty Rain...
is the
only song
still waitin'
to play
on the
jukebox

James Benger

Drip

Those nights she sits alone,
a darkness blacker than
any night could imagine,
if nights could imagine,

but there is something
sentient about the world
in those hours between suns;

that's when the snakes
curl and twist around her insides,
squeezing every final drop
of anything pure,
until any last bit left untainted
is leaked into the nothing.

On those nights,
and most nights are those nights,
she curls on the floor,
wrapping herself around herself
like one of those things,
emulating the enemy that
she knows will win;
it always has won this war.

Infinite

On those nights
we walked the
electric and gas lamp
midnight,
ancient cobblestones
damp with past,
slick with future,
promises and lies,
and all that
luminescent hope,
calls from the periphery,
and the smells of
other lives,
nothing able to change
the fact that
everything always changes,
but the sun was
hours away,
and in the
universe of night,
we were infinite.

Red

We ran through miles of nothing;

tracks and gravel,
broken glass bottles,
jagged, rusted nails
jutting from splintered boards,
what was left of a billboard,
rat or rabbit or maybe chicken bones,
the back cover of a
faded eight-year-old Playboy,
aluminum lids of baby food jars
decrepit enough to predate grandparents,
a note on college-ruled paper,
faded to illegibility;
could've been a love letter,
or a suicide note,
spent bullet casings,
used rubbers,
an unraveled cassette copy of
Licensed to Ill.

We ran for hours
through all those miles of nothing,
searching for anything,
never looking behind.
The sun never set
in any way other than
the most perfect red.

The Druid by Karl Ramberg

Dan Wright

Omit the Logic

Omit the logic
let the world have their myths
When romanticism fades
Reality's a whiskey you can't afford
When you don't have too much
you won't get too far
but everyone wants
to get their dime

Different wavelengths
confuse those
who don't comprehend
Crossroads in Mexico
take you to the same road
where cheap fencing
keeps border patrols company
Trying to focus on your mind
while drunk regulars
pound on guitars
Passion can only take you
so far in a song
but three chords can take you further
Take the pin out of the foundation
watch the building fall
let the new guard build with the remains

Omit all logic
say what you want to say
words are just weapons
that can settle anything
when put in the right order
Violence is their game
because they don't understand yours
as they realize that
a suit of armor to protect themselves
against apple cider vinegar
seems a bit much
but what do you expect
when billy clubs make up
for penis size
When dealing with everyone
from the commander in chief
to your local police officer
omit all logic
omit all reason
and see then if things make sense

The heart is not made to withstand
21st century passism
When it is filled with 20th century passion
Torn between high touch and high tech
Love is in my mind but freedom is in my soul
The voice of poets are powerful enough
to scare fascists

If love of beauty is the path to Hell
then what is the point
of the beauty of Heaven?

World's a Dali painting
wrapped in an Escher staircase
Phobias upload the moment I wake
like a phone that refuses to break
Body is pained but I feel fine
Daily problems I write about never disappear
Pills I'm offered have no effect on me
as freedom stands
beyond comfortable boundaries
Insanity makes sense
when it breaks you
when you omit all logic

House Show

The guitar matches the flame
False endings bring smiles
Dylan poetry used in response
to questions
are met with rolled eyes
Lyrics shine
like champagne and heartache

Claps and snaps
Encourage tales
of honesty confused
for stars
Buddha lamp sheds light
on hipster hi tops
that rub together

Pinky fingers look like lit cigarettes
in a certain light
Beer bottles clank too loudly
as people make whiskey faces
out of embarrassment
Young fanboys now old
wish to travel through time
and dance to suicidal odes
of lost loves

Salt and pepper beards
make conversation with long hair under ski caps
Back row snickers amongst itself
like naughty kids in school
Collage smiles in the dark
Peace in the neighborhood
A drink keeps you company
when you don't know anyone else

Viva La Revolution?

Fingers point in every direction
at the accused
Line between Justice and paranoia
shorter than we think
History books are burned
by those who never read them
in French Revolution atmosphere
Good intentions make for perfect cover
It soon stops being about justice
and becomes people wanting to get rid
of the people we don't like
That's when we're all damaged

Nathanael William Stolte

Grey Brother

I don't recall if I ever knew his name
but we broke bread together
where the guilty or the hopeful
make soup for the loathsome
and some of 'em even treated us with dignity

The soup line was called *Friends of Night People*
The name didn't sit right with me, it still don't

Night People, as if the daylight was not for us
Night People, nocturnal human scourge

The sun goes down and
Ollie Ollie Oxen Free

The invisible crawl out
from under the city's boot-heel
to clean up your discarded aluminum cans

Friend, from the Indo-European root meaning "to love"

I know there is love

Perhaps that's what compels the sweating ladle-maidens
to pour out their boiled compassion into
single servings of salted hope

Perhaps compels the youth groups
to make their monthly pilgrimages
to see god's own children first hand
so they can open their young hearts
invite understanding to move in and
unpack for the long stay

Look for god in the wet eyes
of the veteran begging for change
pocket or otherwise

Look for god in the eyes
that read the runes of the ground
       cracked sidewalk
       flowering weeds
       glittering broken things
You have to work for it
to catch even a glimpse of those darting eyes
but it's worth it, trust me

My grey brother was one of those
brim of his oily ballcap guarding his bowl
dipping stale bread in silence

Never a word
He would walk away with his head down
reading the dead language of earth

Today as I drove
to my own troublesome blessings
I saw my old grey brother
walking tall in his bright yellow
working-man's vest
gathering fallen branches and
other people's carelessness
to collect them in the sturdy bed
of an Olmstead Parks Department Services
crusty John Deere Utility Vehicle
in Delaware Park near Hoyt Lake

It is the doing that we find purpose

Keep your head up grey brother
walk tall in the morning sunlight
and recognize me only
as friend

July Valentine

I stopped offering up
Silent prayers of gratitude &
Began to sing a song of worry
Until I was all out of metaphor so
I headed west in search of the
Nameless madcap riddle &
A secret to divorce from self-pity

In the thrumming
Green heart of America
The blameless eagle
Was splayed in autopsy
In the unthinking lantern light
Of a Kansas City Independence Day

Baptized with mirth &
Sober backyard campfire smoke

In the—
Wiz pop
        Wiz pop
Dazzle shower of
Liquid fireworks
We began to outgrow fear

In the Kansas City slums
They know how to celebrate
Independence
They know what—
Independence means
Not preservation of mercurial freedom
From some imagined foreign oppressor
But freedom
From the bondage—
Of self

-July 4th, 2017

Friday the 13th, October. 2006

That was the autumn the rains
came off the Lake without apology
while trees were yet burdened with leaf

When shelter & comfort of
the burning stream of corn whisky
solace in solidarity & filth

As thundersnow draped
three & a half feet of wet blanket on
the City of Good Neighbors

When the sun quit
me & the city blacked out
but the squats never lost power

the Sabers still
played the Rangers
we go hard in the Nickel City

Tops Market had their lights cut by
overburdened power-lines & filled a
long contractors dumpster with frozen food

We waded in
swam through it
filled the van with—

TGI Fridays mozzarella stick & onion rings
Tony's pizza & enough chicken fingers to feed
the whole subvert army for the already winter

Some people suffered
some died
but it was the trees I felt for

In a formula of
wet snow & surface area
the weight proved too much

It was the oaks that
suffered most   tall & proud
shallow roots & rigid countenance

Scot Young

down a redneck dirt road

where the dirt
meets the blacktop
donna has a camo tarp
stretched over her life
of bags
& boxes &
all she could carry
this is not a common
site in ozark county
nobody goes homeless
on a redneck dirt road
but donna did at 64 years
and 80 pounds
i took her bottled water
asked her what happened
she cried and told me
the stories of every-
thing she had lost
in the last 30 yrs
those that done
her wrong but
she said she believed
in angels
and saints

and god
had a plan
i asked if she could call anyone
i'm out of minutes
she said
bobby is supposed to pick me up

you can use mine if you like
she looked away
an suv drove
by and honked

if you love jesus
she yelled

donna didn't pan
handle didn't have
a sign with *anything will help*
she just sat in a camp chair
off a redneck dirt road
with worn out dreams
smoking a pile of camel
butts
paperback in her lap
waiting for the angels
waiting for the saints
waiting for bobby
to pick her up
and tonight
it is going to rain

white rabbits

at woodstock grace said
it's a new day
a new dawn & sang
the truth is found
to be lies
and all the joy
within you dies

the troubadours
have died
tambourines hang on the wall
the poet's rage slipped
into that good
damn night

we stopped writing
political poems
and forgot all poems are
political
we mimic bukowski
post poems on FB
bitch about trump
and count the comments
like that will change
the world
take the place

of a protest anthem
settle for social media
as the new high
the roadies have
cleared the stage
we stand there
naked
chasing rabbits
and the pill that mother
gives you...

I-435 & Truman Road

there are 3 homeless guys
living under the bridge
on truman road
you can see their
damp blankets
cardboard
water bottles lined up
tucked under the steel
each have a section
for sleep
share the sounds of semis
and sirens on their ceiling
they spend the day
sitting
on plastic buckets
holding signs
    homeless
    hungry
waiting for a window
to roll down
you know the guys
the bucket
the sign
the cold stares
like a dull sun
shining off a winter lake

like waiting
for the ice to freeze
enough for christmas skates
you know the guys
you see them
everyday
through tinted glass
you turn away
like that child
afraid if the ice breaks
you will have to ask
for help

Lamp of Life Karl Ramberg

Zach Fishel

Every Reason / No Reason

The cheap peanut cactus
we bought at Home Depot
blooms when sunlight filters just enough
through the single blackout shade to rip awake
the ceramic morning.
It's so quiet hear you can hear the dew evaporating,
but not before it nourishes some quick bloom
unseen by those afraid to walk into the fire.

Walking at Sunset Crater, as your Wife Laughs at the Word Volcano

Lava is just a minor eon.
The backside of the last

Polaroid left unturned
in the cosmos except

I'm unconcerned
with seeing the other side.

I'm walking this one
on hardened ash,

in the accidental galaxy
of chemical missteps.

Your little dance wears into the teeth
of this black mountain with each laugh.

A pumice stone works itself
Into my boot treads

and my small quiet inferno
dies a little more.

Habit

Sonoran clouds blush awake,
whipping slow daylight into pink meringue
As I work rope around the patio.

Stretches of sky blink to life
like old lawn chairs unfolding
turquoise in the sun.

Formerly daring,
the guideline from our tent
now taut overhead against
The inevitable hummingbirds.

The rope uses a trusted knot,
Wrapped and bleached in the sun,
indifferent to circumstance.
Effortless holding everything together.

Jason Mayer

A Trip Home

It'll be a cold day in Hell before I recognize Missouri!
  - Grandpa Simpson, when told there were 50 states not 49.

These words rang through my head as the 747 began its slow decent across East Saint Louis on Thursday afternoon. I'll never understand why the powers that be decided the best way to introduce people to the Gateway to the West was by passing them over the most wretched part of the city. I could already tell this was going to be a laborious trip... Luckily I had started drinking somewhere over Ohio.

Landing... Luggage... Rental Car... Boring Drive through the country... I had arrived. As I enter the long dusty driveway leading to my parent's house I'm reminded that nothing in this *Show Me State* ever changes, but that's the beauty of it.

I spend a few hours with my mother. She is looking quite ill. The doctors say her liver has progressed from Swiss to more of a blue cheese consistency and is filled with dark sludge. This is all the result of years of hard drinking and the coagulation of some of the most powerful drugs on the planet. She has a tube stuck in her side to help drain her gallbladder, which has grown to the size of a grapefruit. In a normal human they would simply cut the useless thing out, but the fact that she has a heart condition, MS, diabetes, melanoma, a yeast infection and an assortment of other ailments makes the malpractice-weary doctors too queasy to attempt the procedure. I don't blame them. One look at my mom, and you can tell the Reaper is lurking somewhere down the hall. I hate that bastard.

After an uncomfortable hour, I head to my brother's house. Our hellos are short, as we talk almost weekly. We soon settle into some pizza, beer, and a bit of soft-core porn on Skinamax before drifting off to sleep.

Friday

The morning and early afternoon are bleak. More visiting and a bit of computer work. My mother is more coherent today. Now that she has an attentive audience she unloads all her medical horrors on me. Her dissertation is filled with ambulances, doctors, vials, tubes, needles, paddles, Hepatitis C, tests, diagnosis, prognosis, nurses, scoliosis, pain, comas, blood transfusions, dialysis, cancer, and a dizzying amount of other terms. I try to stay attentive and caring, but it's a lot to take in. I must remember to remove these terms from my memory bank before heading back to the civilized world.

At dawn I decide it's time to visit Jack, my best bud from High School and beyond. He has recently returned from a class at the police academy. He's much slimmer than the last time I saw him, and his hair is cut to minimum military specs. He's even clean-shaven, save for a sharply trimmed porn-star mustache. We exchange quick greetings and decide to head out for drinks.

The Rosebud Inn is a small smoky tavern, one of only two in town. Tonight it is filled to capacity with globs of horny middle-aged, Midwestern housewives. Nothing brings out the cows like karaoke. It's only seven and the show is already underway. Strong drink is a must.

The first two hours pass quickly as we exchange stories. A couple others join our party: Doug, a behemoth of a man who is going through the academy with Jack, and Frank, a quiet, meek guy who recently graduated from college with a degree in Political Science, whatever the hell that is.

Soon the lights are lowered and the singers become even more earnest. The mix of songsters is maddening. The first is a sad old man bellowing *Always on My Mind*. He's not accompanied by anyone, and the song sounds even more depressing as he sings to a hole in the wall.

Next up is a 40-something lady in tight black jeans and an even tighter red shirt. She has jet-black hair that is slicked back in a ponytail. She looks like an aged version of a Robert Palmer girl from the *Simply Irresistible* video. In a certain light she looks deceptively pretty, in a dirty *Mrs. Robinson* sort of way. This could be exacerbated with more powerful drinking glasses.

She gives a raucous rendition of Pat Benatar's *Love is a Battlefield*, and I swear she is pointing her hip gyrations my way.

The third victim is a strange, young, wiry boy affectionately named Rappin' Rob. Rob has coke-bottle glasses and a gangly demeanor about him. While certainly obnoxious, the young man gives a decent performance of *I Told You Mamma* by EMNEM. The crowd has mixed reactions. Most of the women try to act hip by flailing their arms and mouthing the chorus, some even get up to dance. The dumbass rednecks begin their murmurs, "This ain't county," "I don't care for that afro music," "Somebody ought to talk to that boy," and "Ain't that what they call a Wigger?"

However the best part of Rob's performance isn't the fact that he can actually sing, the crazed women, or the gaggle of half-drunk heckling racists. The best part is the strange troll attached to his every move. The Troll is an odd looking girl standing just over four and a half feet tall, sporting a bowl haircut and wearing a Cat-In-The-Hat striped shirt. The beast spasms and hops wildly around Rob while flashing gang signs. The show is a spectacle.

At this point, we decide to pick up the drinking pace. The singers rotate through in droves, and I find myself enjoying the strangeness of it all.

Finally, Frank gets up and gives an awful rendition of *Here Without You* by Three Doors Down. Throughout the song he seems to be singing directly at the Troll, as she swaps spit with Rappin' Rob. Jack confirms this saying, "She's his ex. She dumped him about a week ago. He said it was mutual, but I am not so sure."

After the song, Frank flops down in his chair looking positively somber. A few quiet moments pass before Rob,

Troll in tow, walks up to the table. They begin a
polite banter with Frank, which is a bit disconcerting.
The Troll appears to be humping Rob's leg throughout
the conversation and Frank is almost sugary as he goes
through his pleasantries. The conversation ends with
Frank inviting the duo to sit with us.

For some inexplicable reason I become irate at this notion.
I have no vested interest in the situation. I don't know
Frank from Adam, and it's really none of my business.
Still, I decide that action must be taken. "What the fuck
are you thinking! Do you really want those two freaks
sitting with us? She's your ex, He's a cocky ass. And besides
that they're both being disrespectful!" I say, displaying a
look of utter contempt.

"Well, what was I supposed to do?" Is all he can say.

"I'll tell you what you're supposed to do… Tell them to
fuck off. You're an educated man for Pete's sake! Use that
big brain of yours to think up something better than
'join our table so you can make me look like a loser and
everyone else feel like idiots.'"

"I can't do that. I don't want to make a scene, and I don't
want her to think my friends are making me alienate her.
We share a lot of the same friends."

This infuriates me. "Unacceptable! And I don't even
fucking know you!" I scream as the Wonder Twins
approach with drinks in hand. I decide to take matters
into my own hands, bolstered by pure principal.

I turn on the approaching duo. "This guy doesn't seem to mind the fact that his ex wants to sit next to him and make out with Slim Shady here, but I'm just a little uncomfortable with the whole idea. I've been out of touch with hillbilly etiquette for a while, so I'm not sure at what point it became acceptable to pull this kind of shit. Why don't you two take your happy asses back across the bar and make mad monkey love somewhere else. Let the poor sap drink in peace."

It is about this time that I realize the drink is beginning to take hold. Running on testosterone, I decide to grab the Robert Palmer girl and whirl her around the dance floor. The song is *Baby Got Back*. Glory be!

Saturday

The next morning I wake up feeling energized. This is quickly eviscerated, as one by one my family comes to visit.

First comes my grandmother, a ray of hope. I've always liked my grandma. She's the hardest working person I know. The epitome of a good woman. She's always been the Queen Mother. She's a veteran of two 20-year factory jobs and even worked part time in another factory for five extra years past her first two retirements. She never made more than a couple pennies over minimum wage, but still managed to raise four boys and a girl. Plus she found a way to invest enough money to retire on. Un-fucking-believable.

Grandma and I speak briefly about the new house she's having built until we are interrupted by the arrival of my mom's oldest friend Dana.

Dana is an overly bitter woman, who I have never liked. Somehow she conned my guilt-riddled father into hiring her to take care of the house while he is away hauling loads as a truck driver. She feels almost deified by her new position. Since she's been my mother's friend for decades, she knows everything about my family and has no shortage of opinions about how they should live their lives.

We exchange lethargic hellos and she begins her constant stream of bitching. As always, her ire is directed towards "The Clan" as she calls my father's side of the family. Her rundown of random family members begins:

My Brother: He's got a good job, but he's whoring around with tons of young women. Dana is disappointed. I disagree… live boy live.

My Uncle Thomas: He's a base drunk who is ruining his kids' lives. Not to mention he's a horrible husband and all around asshole. Dana is disappointed. I whole-heartedly agree.

Thomas' Wife Jan: She is a fool for staying with Thomas and is close to losing her teaching job because things at home are causing her to yell at the kids. Dana is disappointed. I'm ambivalent.

My Cousin Jim, Thomas' Son: He's a bully, boozer, womanizer and he's going to end up like his father. Dana is disappointed. I'm not so sure, he's still young.

My Grandpa: Years of a steady diet of Sun Drop and Old Crow whiskey have taken their toll. He weighs a svelte 113 pounds and does nothing but watch Jerry Springer all day and reminisce about his days in the Army all night. Dana is disappointed. God Bless the Irish bastard, a hero among men.

My Cousin Sam: He is a college graduate with a masters and two bachelor's degrees. He recently enlisted in the Navy Reserves on a special program, and he should be making millions by now, not just starting his life. Dana is disappointed. Leave the man be.

My Dad: As the oldest sibling, he's supposed to be the leader of the pack. It's his fault that everyone is so screwed up. Dana is disappointed. I'm starting to get pissed off.

My Grandma: She lets too many people walk all over her. She lets her kids take advantage of her and my grandpa doesn't appreciate her. Dana is disappointed. Shut the fuck up!

I escape the madness by faking a phone call… Better to pull off a rouse than punch the old woman in the face. I retreat to the spare bedroom and decide to catch a nap. When I wake up, my mother's live-in caretaker arrives… enter Amy, Snow White's white trash cousin.

Amy is 30, a stringy blonde and very thin. She is quite attractive when standing quietly and looking straight ahead, but her beauty is tarnished when she starts talking and moving about. Her voice is whiskey harsh and she has a horrid smoker's cough. There is a strange stutter to all her movements, almost epileptic at times. She is wearing tattered skin-tight jeans and a titty-tight T-Shirt that reads, "I'm Baaaad," with a smirking sheep underneath. One hand is holding a Natural Light and the other is linking the chain from her current cigarette to a new one. Her eyes are glassy and distant… must be high. In any other place she would be a street hag, a burnout, a no-good nick at the least. In this ass-backwards area, she's practically marriage material. Yes my friends, an honest-to-god hillbilly goddess.

I sit in the living room pretending to watch TV as she tends to my mother's needs. I can hear my mom recounting my heroics. To hear her version of the story, I'm next in line to be King of All. Wealthy, hansom, responsible, educated, well-traveled, hung like a mule, the works. God bless all mothers.

She exits and room and turns toward the living room, blushing at the sight of me. Who can blame her? She heads to the kitchen and starts cleaning, and I stroll into the adjoining sunroom. We roll through a few awkward intros and settle into an easy conversation about my mom's health. The banter quickly moves to partying, and I invite her to a join me and the boys for a romp in the big city.

On With the Show

It's nine in the evening and the car is loaded. I'm driving; Amy is squeezed in between Jack and Frank in the back seat and my uncle James is in the passenger seat.

My uncle James recently finished a fifteen year stint in a Texas federal pen for stealing an Army jeep and knifing a filthy heathen. He looks like an anorexic version of Grizzly Adams, with a potbelly and mean cocaine habit. Nice man though.

The thirty-mile ride is fast and furious. I only slow down twice. Once at the curve where a friend of mine in high school named Paul died in a car crash. The other is to stop at the QuickMart to pick up beer, beef jerky, and breath mints. We arrive in tact and park outside a warehouse-looking bar. Jack insists that this is the greatest tavern in the region.

Inside the place is packed with a good mix, seventy percent women thirty percent men. It's a square, uncomfortably-lit room with a long bar on one side and stage to the left. We find the best seats available, which are the worst. Luck be damned. The band is still setting up, and I decide to start the night with shots. This isn't my normal routine, but I'm on vacation. Jack and I down shots of Jim Beam and grab a beer.

Set 1

The band starts playing at ten sharp. It's a motley bunch that goes by the name, Steel Piglets. A middle-aged goat named Brent fronts the group and the lead guitarist is a friend of mine from the past named Scott. They are surprisingly good for a cover band and even play a bit of the new stuff. They start with *Mustang Sally, Pink Houses,* and *Brown Eyed Girl.* After that comes *Sweet Home Alabama,* which makes me think of my friend Steve. God how he hates Lynyrd Skynyrd. What a loser.

Our small group begins to grow as the night progresses. Jack, Frank, James, Amy, and I are joined by a guy named Bird (our rich computer-wielding friend from Saint Louis) and two other girls plus their companions whom I don't know. I soon find out that one of the girls is Frank's new main squeeze. She has conveniently invited her ex-husband along for the date, which perplexes me at first. I shake it off and decide that Frank is one fucked up son of a bitch.

The drinks start to flow at this point. I feel like a cash cow, but I can afford it at these prices. One dollar per beer and another dollar for a shot. Beer, shot, beer, shot, beer, shot, etc. This continues until the first slow song, which traditionally denotes the end of a set for honky-tonk bands. The song is *Desperado,* and Amy demands to dance. It's not until this moment that I realize the girl has been getting a bit frisky for the past few drinks. We spin a few silent, slow circles and she gives me a doe-eyed look. I need more alcohol.

Set 2

During the break the lights come back up for some unknown reason and everyone seems afraid of their drinks. We sit and chat nervously until the room goes dim again. Recharged, Jack and I make a command decision to switch to boilermakers. There's no since in splitting up the beer and whiskey at this point. The idea is simple, drop and drink. Being frugal and lazy, we buy three pitchers of beer and twelve shots. The tab is a cool forty dollars, including tip.

We set ourselves at one end of the table and guard our stash. With the discipline of monks we begin our chore: fill a glass to the brim, drink it down a quarter of the way, drop a shot, pound. This is repeated three times.

Set 3

I'm not sure at what point I get the happy feet, but I decide it's time to dance. I feel like John Travolta in Saturday Night Fever. I'm sure it's ugly to behold, but being one of only three dudes on the dance floor (and the only one under forty), I have my pick of the litter. There are hordes of felines all around. I bull my way into a group and gyrate up and down the line.

Set 4

Luckily I've sweated off a few ounces of go juice and am ready for a break. I take my seat and use the turned up lights to scout the crowd. Horrible! I demand to know whose stupid idea it is to brighten the lights this late in the game. Terrible! A complete shock to the system. Girls that seemed pleasant in the dim, now look frumpy and haggish. I begin to become paranoid as I spy eyes glaring back at me. DO I LOOK THIS HORRID? I quickly call for the barmaid to bring three more pitchers and twelve more shots, stat.

Jack has been making the rounds trying to determine if there are any ladies in the house that he is not related to, and reports for duty as soon as the drinks arrive. The band starts with *Take It Easy* and we go back to our boilermaker routine. This time the medicine seems to have an adverse effect. The room grows hollow and tube-like and I start to feel hazy. Sensing danger, Amy rallies the troops and calls for a retreat.

The car ride home goes by in a blur: James drives, I'm shotgun, and Amy is once again squeezed in between Jack and Frank. Conversations abound, but the only thing I can make out is Jack screaming, "You crazy bitch!" This should have been an omen.

Sunday

I wake up the next morning at my parent's house, dry mouthed and oppressed. I'm fully clothed and sweating profusely. As I begin to focus, I realize that Amy is tucked neatly under my arm in a fetal ball. I lie still for a moment trying to recount last night's actions. There is a dark spot in my mind from when we left the bar to my current position. I quickly surmise that there is little chance I did anything immoral. I was simply too far gone.

A knock at the door pulls Amy from her slumber. It's my mother asking if I'd like some breakfast. What a sneaky critter.

Amy flies out of bed like she's been stung by a cattle prod. The scene is hilarious; the look on her face is priceless. I simply smirk at her. She fumbles aimlessly around the room trying in futility to find her pants and gain some semblance of control. Eventually she shoots me a guilt-ridden look and smashes through the door holding a pile of her clothes. White trash turned yellow.

I spend the rest of the day recuperating. After further investigation and a few eyewitness accounts, I determine that my suspicions were correct – I had bedded alone. The sleazy harlot must have crept into my rack sometime during the night. Looking for a father figure no doubt.

Monday

Monday is a slow day. I watch *The Quiet Man* and entertain fantasies of humping plumb Irish maddens in the days of yore. Giant white snowflakes start falling at around noon. By six there is more than a foot of powder on the ground. Sleep is peaceful.

Tuesday

The morning brings a glorious view of a winter wonderland. The woods behind my parent's house are covered in a beautiful white blanket. I get a call from work saying that my boss is going to be fired. Serves him right, the lazy bastard. He was the worst kind of man. Former politician, eight years in the making. He was the type who assessed the job (poorly), barked incoherent orders and slumped behind his desk in pious indignation. Then while others worked feverously for the good of all, he would take the credit and pass the blame. Awful, greasy, sleazebag.

I decide not to overthink the situation. It's a problem for another day. Plus, my mother's cat is starting to get to my allergies.

Wednesday – Thursday

Slow uneventful days. I spend most of the time visiting with my mother and doing work on the computer. The white blanket has turned to an ugly brown sludge and I refuse to leave the safety of shelter.

The cat is really starting to bother me. I spot it in the corner and stomp on its tail.

Friday

I'm starting to get restless. I've had minimal amounts of booze since Saturday. I'm tired of playing the good son, but the party crowd is working late this evening. Wait until tomorrow they say.

My allergies are starting to get out of control. I start actively hunting for the cat to exact my revenge, but the wily feline is on to me.

In the late afternoon James and Amy appear from James' room in the basement. Amy has trouble looking me in the eyes and both of them smell of herb.

I immediately snap to and begin barking orders. Get your coats, I need a drink. We head to The Old Roller Mill, which reportedly has a special event going on. A special event at the Mill! This I've got to see.

We arrive at the Mill in all our glory. The Mill is an old grain mill built in the late 1800s that has been converted into a bar and grill. It's built of old worm-eaten logs and has a grimy look and feel to it. There are only six people in the place and all of them stare at us like we're from Neptune. Damn cretins.

We slurp lukewarm beer and nibble on chicken fingers for a while until we determine there is little truth to the whole "Special Event" rumor. False advertising at its worse.

We give up hope and head to the Rosebud Inn. I stop at the door trying to assess the scene. It's a complete recreation of last Friday. A fucking time warp. The same people, in the same seats, wearing the same clothes, drinking the same drinks, singing the same sad songs.

Try as I may, I can't seem to get the drinks to go down. I have a look of disgust on my face and a lump in my throat. I'm starting to feel superior, which I know is dangerous. I indignantly refuse to dance with anyone, especially the Robert Palmer girl. I'm not sure what my problem is — must be the company I'm with. Fuck this, sleep is more pleasant. Where's my friend Brandon when I need him, a two-fisted Irishman. A real drinking companion.

Saturday

I wake up full of piss and vinegar. The piss is drained into the toilette, but the vinegar can only be neutralized with alcohol. I sense from the start, this is going to be a rugged, manly day, filled with debauchery and base activity. Lofty goals.

A small damper enters the picture when my dad rolls in from weeks of hard big-rig driving. He's dog tired, but determined to spend some quality time with me. I figure it best to take the man to lunch, fill his bell, and tuck the poor soul into bed.

We head to the only Mexican joint within 50 miles. It's an experimental place owned by a man named Randy Chuckworth.

My dad is the first person to ask me about my life since I've been in town. I rattle through a few details and quickly change the subject back to his side. He goes through his version of my mother's health problems, which is always more informative and to the point. After that he gives me a briefing on their financial situation, which is abysmal.

The medical bills have been piling up, and they now owe more than $53,000 with more to come. My dad just shakes it off. He has already devised a plan to pay it all off in a timely manner. He just finishes his lunch and refuses to let me pay for the check. True grit personified.

We head back to the house. I convince my dad to get some sleep and promise to visit with him more in the morning before I leave.

I shake off the bleakness and dart to Jack's for a preflight. It's only seven when I arrive, but Jack is ready to go. Wasting no time, we guzzle a few gulps of Bushmill's straight from the bottle and head down the road. Jack looks a bit hazy. He's been up for almost thirty hours between work, the police academy, and work again. No worries, he's Irish and drinking.

The Quick Mart serves as our restaurant of choice, and we gorge on stale pizza slices, chicken wings, and Budweiser. We're back on the road in no time.

We arrive at the same warehouse bar as last Saturday and barge through the door, men of purpose and conviction. Shining stars.

We skip the How Ya Do's and rush to the bar. Double for him, double for me. It's a bourbon and Coke night. We each grab a stool, plunge down the drinks and turn back to the bear of a man tending the bar. Jack orders this time… two martinis.

This is a first for me, and I glare sourly at the small clear substance supporting a toothpick-speared olive. The contents could be contained in a Dixie cup. Not schooled in the finer points of martini drinking, I shoot the wad. My throat immediately closes and my eyes fill with water. I can barely breathe. "What the hell! Is that fucking rubbing alcohol?" I squeak at Jack. He gives me a scolding look and chastises me for not sipping the thing properly. I flip him the bird and order another double bourbon and Coke. The planets are realigned.

Time to make our social rounds. We pass through small clumps of people, each containing at least one or two people we know. No real conversations are had, just a lot of smiling and nodding. I've never been very talkative, and reunion situations make me a bit queasy. We finally make it to our table and take our seats.

Tonight we're joined again by Doug, Bird, Frank, and the two floozies from last Saturday. This time the two girls are joined by only one guy. Frank's lady is working hard to repair the damage from last week's ex-husband debacle. Frank seems surly and proud. It figures that the impotent fucker would wait until the enemy leaves camp to take a stand.

It takes me a while, but I realize three new additions have joined the party. They're all sitting at the far end of the table. For some strange reason Rappin' Rob and the Troll have made a showing. They're in deep conversation about the cosmic differences between Frank's Hard Lemonade and Smirnoff Ice. The other newbie is a twenty-something girl with dark brown hair, a cute face, and educated eyes. She has the look of a country maiden – ample breast, plump rear, and tight waist… a must have accessory for any vacationing city man.

The group is awkwardly silent, and I decide to announce my presence. "What the Hell!" I say obscenely loud for no apparent reason. Rappin' Rob, thinking my phrase is directed at him, cowers in defense. I simply ignore him and continue puffing out my chest and call for a toast. Everyone at the table holds up their glasses. The King of All has arrived.

Forgetting rank, Jack orders four more drinks and introduces me to the Maiden Ashley. She flashes me a shy smile and flips her hair. She's on to the game.

I decide to take the coy route, and settle into a rhythm. I drink moderately for a while and survey the group. Doug and Bird have picked out two targets in the corner. One is slightly chubby but fair, the other is bone skinny with great hair. They work feverishly on a plan. Frank stares at the soft-core sex show between Rob and the Troll. He doesn't even glance at his new fling, who is beginning to sour. Jack has returned to his social rounds. He has always been the popular one.

This leaves me with the Maiden Ashley. The other Bulls sensing my dominance have cleared the arena. She gives me a short run down of her life – single, still in college, 24, nice parents, wants to be a florist, loves adventure. Easy pickings.

I give her my stats, leaving out a few choice details, and buy her a couple drinks. Cranberry vodka and shot of hot damn. Bourbon and Coke for me.

Shortly after, the Steel Piglets begin their first set. Ashley is keen on dancing, but I'll have none of it until I'm properly lubed. Frank is drafted for the job. I feel a bit slighted, but the pore slob needs some hope in his life.

Jack returns from his rounds, but the devil has committed a mortal sin. His grubby hands grip a tray of tequila shots. I feel a knot welling in my stomach – impending doom.

The tray is crowded with doubles. I shake off my conscience and sling back one of the fat goblets. The liquid goes down easy, and I grab another. A little voice whispers something about lessons from the past, but it's drowned out by a second splash in my throat.

Fueled by machismo, the men in the group steam through the tray. The Maiden Ashley looks disapproving at our callous disregard for reason. Her smile is fading.

I decide to humor her with a dance. We hit the floor in time to catch the start of *Gimme Three Steps*. I perform horridly, but Ashley is all giggles. She has a seductive hip sway, which mesmerizes me for a while. I feel clear and happy. I'm in the eye of the storm.

We return to the table and I feel absolutely giddy. I notice a group of friends I went to school with sitting at a table in the corner. I strut over, using my city-man walk and greet everyone with the usual, "What the Hell!"

The group goes something like this: Darren – a short, stocky geek of a man, who owns a sign making business; Jack – a skinny farm boy, who recently took over his father's dairy farm; Jen – a slutty but nice girl, who works in the local hat factory; and Laura – a pretty, sweet girl that I dated in high school for a short while.

We exchange abbreviated life stories, which I only half listen to. The only one I'm really interested in is Laura because she was always an innocent girl and one of the few people I truly considered a friend. She's always been better than the rest of us degenerates. I had hoped that the world had been kind to her, but that was too much to ask for in this forsaken land.

It turns out Laura works as a veterinarian's assistant for Doc Blackwell, a respectable man. She's been dating a guy by the name of Max Wiserman for the past few years, and they are engaged to be married in the summer. This perplexes me. I have always known Max to be a complete asshat.

Laura fidgets throughout the conversation and keeps glancing at Max, who is sitting alone a few tables over. He looks drunk and surly. After a short while, Laura excuses herself and joins her mate.

Darren, Jack, and Jen immediately dump the rest of the story on me. It turns out Laura started dating Max a couple years ago a few months after he finished drug rehab. They even met at church. Now that he's relapsed, she feels obligated to stand by her man. They also point out the dark circle under her left eye (I must have must have been distracted by her size D chest). I digest it all and swig another drink. The storm is rising.

Jack is beside himself as I relate the story to him. He's always been a more honorable man than I. He immediately calls Doug over and gives him the rundown. Doug stands nearly seven feet tall and weighs an easy 300 pounds.

He is a calm man and drinks very sparingly. He is not pleased with the news. A few years back he put his stepfather in the hospital over similar circumstances. The news travels around our table, and I feel the posy getting restless.

I've never been a big fighter. Mainly because I'm not one of those guys that can claim he's never been taken down. In my experience, the more drunk of two combatants almost always winds up on his ass, and this usually puts me at a disadvantage. However, I've learned to compensate for this by keeping a stash of informed bullies at my back before heading into battle. In this instance I find the bully brigade more than ready to rush the bastard.

I calm the gang down, as we spy on Max. He's oblivious to his surroundings and appears to be growling at Laura, who in turn pouts into her diet Coke. A few moments pass, and I can feel the pit in my stomach start to subside. I sip on a drink and contemplate my next actions. No need to be rash.

That's when things start to boil. Max suddenly grabs Laura's arm, grits his teeth and seethes something at her. She winces at his grip and cowers as if ready to be punched. The scene is almost too much for Doug to bear, and I decide I better do something fast.

I tell Jack to follow me and signal for Doug to dance with his newfound honey near our target. Jack and I stroll up to Max and Laura's table wearing polite smiles. We say hello to Max and grab a seat. He seems a little uncomfortable with our arrival, but keeps the conversation civil. Jack does all of the talking, relating his story and mine.

All the while I survey the table, looking for potential weapons and pitfalls… beer bottles, tumblers, and a dirty, fake alabaster ashtray are all that sit on the table.

Eventually, Jack eases the conversation towards Max's recent stint in rehab. Max's face reddens and he's obviously feeling attacked. He tries to avoid the questions, but Jack is relentless.

Laura has remained quiet throughout the conversation, but this new banter is making her nervous. I calmly pass her twenty bucks and ask her to pick up a round for the table. She nods, gets up slowly, and turns to the bar.

Jack waits until she's out of earshot, then charges. "What's with that ring under Laura's eye, it looks like someone punched her?" he blurts out. Max is silent. "And that red mark on her arm looks like it might bruise." Max is silent. "You know Jason and I were good friends with Laura in school. We haven't seen her in a while, and I'm disappointed that she seems to be getting hurt all the time. What's up with that?" Max is silent.

Sensing the hostility rising, Max clenches his fist and shuffles his feet. His eyes narrow and he pushes his chair back. He starts to stand up but Doug rushes into action and kicks his chair from behind. The seat slams into Max's calves and he slams back into the chair. He glares back at Doug, but seeing his size, he decides not to make another attempt a standing. He turns back to Jack who is still waiting patiently for answers.

During the start of this parley, the pit in my stomach returns, and for some strange reason a line from the Talking Heads song *Psycho Killer* starts ringing in my head.

I sing the line "I hate people when they're not polite" under my breath as I reach out for Max's head. It's a glorious motion that seems to flow in slow motion. Max, turning his focus from Jack's inquisition toward the sound of my awful tenor, watches dumbly as my hand comes up behind his head. In a quick fluid motion I slam his head down on the table, centering it squarely on one edge of the alabaster ashtray.

His head snaps back and he sits in a daze. A thin line of blood in a distinct "U" shape caused by the cigarette slot immediately starts welling up in the center of his forehead.

It was a sucker move, but I can't seem to muster up much guilt for my actions. If I'd been any drunker I wouldn't have been able to pull it off; any more sober and I wouldn't have had the nerve.

Jack remains calm and serious. He suddenly adopts a parental tone, "Now I think we all know that Laura is a special person, and she just can't be hurt anymore. We're trusting you to make sure that doesn't happen. We're going to make a point of checking up on her a little more often.

Doug back there is graduating with me next month from the police academy, and he lives just down the block from Laura's house."

Justice done, Max simply sits dumbfounded as Laura returns with the drinks. She passes the drinks around, and Jack snatches up his drink and the Budweiser that was meant for Max. "Max is feeling a little under the weather. I think he needs to go home," I say to Laura. She looks at her fiancée, who turns his face away and starts fumbling with his jacket. I hug Laura goodbye and ask her to share her contact info with Jack. She does and they leave.

I swagger back to the main table, starting to feel the effects of the tequila… teeth numb, unquenchable thirst, the room moving under me, slight paranoia. I smile stupidly as Jack recounts our heroics. The crowd is thrilled. I look to Maiden Ashley for approval. She has a white look about her, but is obviously impressed with the event. I feel like a champion, a tequila soaked Hercules.

The bartender comes barreling up to the table, and I'm certain she's here to toss the lot of us. Instead she's carrying a tray of shots courtesy of Darren, Jack and Jen. I scour the tray and see nothing but skinny vials of tequila. The stomach will not approve. I grab a shot, hold it up as a toast to the thankful trio and shoot it down.

Maiden Ashley will just have to bed alone.

Sunday

I awake to a cold sweat in the spare bedroom of my parent's house. I try in vain to recount the last few hours of the night before – another black spot haunts my mind. I'm comforted by the facts that once again I am fully clothed and I have Ashley's name and number written on my hand. The room is clean, no vomit. My head is pounding.

I only have a couple hours before it's time to leave for the airport, so I reluctantly take to my chores of showering and packing. The goodbyes seem to last an eternity, especially with my mother. She cries a lot and tells me how proud she is. If only she knew – but of course she does. I hug my dad and tell him I will call him in a couple days.

I wave a final goodbye and head out. The airport is dreary and quiet. Everyone shuffling in their proper lanes as they are herded to their assigned seats.

I find my aisle seat and situate myself for the peaceful flight home. Just as I'm preparing to nod off I spy a medium-sized young lady making her way back to her seat. She has a distinct Midwestern sway, large ass, big breasts and stringy blond hair. All of this screams of white trash, but the point is driven home by the fact that she is wearing black sweatpants with the word "JUICY" printed in large white letters across her hindquarters.

My god they're exporting the stuff.

Dianne Borsenik

Finding Myself Inside a Quentin Tarantino Movie in Cleveland at Four O'clock in the Afternoon

It's four o'clock in the afternoon, and we're the first
ones through the door at Porco's Lounge and Tiki Room—
at least, that's what we'd planned, but we're met by a
man-bunned film crew setting up their gear. I sit in our

usual booth, order a Fogg Cutter. Wild surf music rips
through the speakers—Dick Dale's *Misirlou*—and I can
hear owner Stefan telling one of his stories, which then
segues into an interview with *Destination Cleveland.*

I order another drink. It arrives, dry ice making it smoke
and bubble like a witch's cauldron. The interview ends.
Stefan saunters over to *Walk Don't Run,* slams his wallet
on the table. It's the one from *Pulp Fiction*—you know

the one, the Bad MF one—and everything turns surreal.
All those little tiki-faced mugs bore into me with unblinking
eyes. The skeleton that swings from the rafters swigs his
never-ending string of LED light. The question WWDD—

What Would Don (the Beachcomber) Do—hangs over the
bar, and the smell of Pusser's Rum is in the air. *Tequila*
hits the speakers, and that's when I realize: I'm in a Quentin
Tarantino movie, and my drink is ready for its close up.

Seeing Jim Morrison in Giant Eagle on the First Day of Autumn

It's the hottest it's been
on the first day of autumn
since 1895, and 92 degrees
Fahrenheit calls for ice
cream and alcohol

to celebrate. At the State
Liquor Agency in Giant Eagle,
Jim Morrison, reincarnated,
scans the bar code
on the bottle and tells me

to insert my chip. He
doesn't smile the entire
time; he just tosses back
a lock of hair and purses
those iconic lips.

I can't help myself. *Do you
know who The Doors are?*
I ask him, and he
meets my eyes. *I've
heard of them,* he lies.

*You look like the lead
singer,* I tell him, hoping
once home he'll Google it,
discover the music, see
for himself proof that

fifty years ago, he
walked the earth as a god,
wore black leather, sang
Come on, baby, light my fire,
ignited a generation.

This Can't Be Oklahoma

—after "Yoder Farm," watercolor on canvas, by William David Simon

This can't be Oklahoma, not
this farm, so desolate, so sterile, so
barren of cow. This can't be Oklahoma,
where it's possible to see more
cows in one day than in one's
entire life outside Oklahoma—
coffee-colored, nut-brown cows,
cows in plenitude, cows ubiquitous.

This can't be Oklahoma, and
this can't be April, when the cattle
have calved and every blade of
viridescent grass is called into play
to pasture the cows, to nourish
the cows, to cradle the cows when they
tire of eating and fold their legs. There's
too much undisturbed grass for April.

No, this can't be Oklahoma, not
these whitewashed outbuildings
surely filled with pale ambient light
and the petrichor of the morning's rain,
dust sifting into empty corners. No
bellows, no snorts, no stamping hooves
inhabit here. This place, so *unbovine*,
can't be Oklahoma.

The Cedar by Karl Ramberg

Jeanette Powers

The Creek Calls the Storm Waters

Drizzle, sprinkle, torrent, mist, palpitations of wind, clouds just can't anymore and fall, bit by tiny bit. They fall at our feet, they cover every inch, they leave no being untouched in their relentless downpour. The water soaks the ground, the water lays on top of the water and pushes the water to a very specific spot: the Lagrangian, this is a physics word but we watch it every time the creek calls the storm waters. The Langrangian is the place that is both the lowest and the *downhilliest*, it is the place of least action. Like it or not, all the waters speak to one another and heed the call of the creek, rushing to her borders, fattening her up like a caterpillar about to burst into new life, and transform from fluffy white to raging creek, from river into delta into ocean, and right back around again.

How do the waters know which direction to head? Or that they should head anywhere at all? They are compelled and called by the shape of the mountain and the weight of the spinning earth. They are falling like circus clowns and acrobats, both willy-nilly and with unbelievable grace. The waters do join, the waters do fall, the waters batter and rage and cascade, the waters move mountains and make slow caves and holes in rocks the creek gives me. The Lagrangian doesn't just tell the rain's story of going home, but describes all motion as we know it. Everything, like it or not, is somehow falling along the path of least action, conserving energy, the universe doesn't get a tax refund and doesn't owe the government at the end of the year. Nothing is wasted, but everything is spent.

This is a truth of our lives, like it or not, each of our choices are along the path of least action. This paints a new storm over your past, your memories, your loves. This person was the lowest and *downhilliest* person you could love, this job took the minimal amount of energy and consumed you completely. Some of us are clouds, some are snowcaps, some are rainstorms, some are creeks guiding drops into rivers, some are oceans, some of us are the unlikely moment of evaporation and are lifted against reason skyward, we're all destined to be each of these things sometimes.

Today Rocklayer Creek is gregarious, playful. My son and I walk through the pouring rain with Puppy Moss to see what seven inches of rain in a single day looks like. The water that touched the barely soles of my feet is a bit beyond ankle deep at the crossing in the lower meadow. The crossing which was a hands length across is now my body's length across. I stand in the center of the rushing gusher. The number of gallons per hour crossing my feet would wrap the Earth three and a half times if gallons were miles. It's the weight of 14 elephants. I stand still as I look up creek and back down while being soaked through with the pelting ocean brought to middle Missouri. At the swimming hole in the creek where the down of the two Ozark mountains meet, the pool is long gone, having grown wide and deep and all the dry bed spots are now coursing complete to the open arms of the Gasconade River.

Something is calling the water. The water feels it and reacts purely. There's no stopping it.

Something is calling me. I feel it and am told a million names and reasons for it. The pull of the fall into my line of motion has a trajectory that I'm innocent to, just as the water reacts, I react. The delta is always a surprise. The delta is inevitable. My father's family calls it *God*, in *Jesus'* name *amen*. The hard atheists call it *chance*, in Darwin's name *beagle*. The Buddhists call it *Zen*, in no name *nothing*. The existentialists call it *anguish*, in Camus' name *laugh*. The physicists call it *Lagrangians*, in Feynman's name *you are the easiest person to fool*. Each of every us feels the pull and attempts to put a name to it, because that is what we do. Today I will call it *turtle/snake*, because one name is as good as the next if we all know the feeling we are talking about.

I want to emphasize that we are made of smaller particles. Our big-body-compact connections-made molecules-bonded bodies don't have much room for new atoms to make their way in. We've done a real number on taking up all the space within. Our atoms have all their electrons, except for in the brain, where electricity reigns and synapses fire and information is transferred like wildfire, all zapping brainstorm all the time with raindrops and rivulets and creeks and rivers and oceans of ideas all gone delta on the calculus of thinking.

Electrons carry information. That's how cell phones and computers work, the electricity of the thing ones and zeros its way from my tap-tapping fingers to the screen across continents to a printer to a bookstore where you exchange some small currency for the words that excited my neurons enough to spend minimal energy typing them up for you. Our bodies are activated by energy, our bodies carry information. Our bodies emanate signals, they are called *de Broglie* Waves. Our bodies exhibit a particle-wave duality. Even without computers and typing and sending ideas over email, we vibrate waves from our being. We are transmitters, like it or not.

There is a radio inside of you that hears these waves. There is a CB (citizen's band) radio microphone that is broadcasting your story, your electrons leave so many marks on the world around you. We dial in or tune out, but it doesn't stop the stories from finding their way downhill to the river. Like it or not, your mark is left on the world and the world is marking you, signaling you, vibrating you constantly. There is not one moment that you aren't shook by the thunder of the existence of the whole universe.

(I know you feel it. You probably are afraid of it. You probably stay in out of the rain and don't enter raging creeks or throw yourself into rivers or court snakes. All perfectly sensible things to avoid, truly, for your kind of least action. I understand why you are afraid of someone wild picking up on your wavelengths. Maybe you are afraid of who you might be.)

Among the *skepticaliest* skeptics, they almost would agree on one thing: energy is neither created or destroyed, instead it only changes form. We emanate energy, energy cannot be destroyed. Energy is information. It's at least *possible* that there exists information which cannot be destroyed. Praise Jesus, Darwin, Buddha, Camus and Feynman!

Maybe the waves of the thoughts of the electrical systems of our brains continue on and outward and shape and inform the universe and, like it or not, we ourselves can detect and feel, I mean *feel*, the histories and stories of every is and every thought that has ever been and thought in the all of all of infinity. Maybe there's a storm of truth in the ether falling down on us, drenching us in all of the knowledge of eternity and in that way, we achieve eternal life.

If we stop with the nervous tics, if we stop biting our lips and picking, picking. If we tune in to the vibrations of our bodies and then, listen to how our own outreaching reacts and connects and intermingles with the rest of the totality. If we turn off the noise and hear the world. If we adventure into the world and explore the inner frequency. If we be like the tree, and grow to the fullest given what we're given. If we rush to the delta. If we stand in the pouring rain.

Then we'll feel the pull down our creek and not be able to help but know which way to go.

Steve Brightman

Aphrodite Put Her Faith in the Golden Apple to Distract Her from a Corrugated Heart

In the dark,
everything
is ugly and
everything
is gorgeous.

Things of which
we do not speak
inch nearer and
upward to find
any light or any
source of water.

Love is then
cut into flesh
in reverse,
so that when
blood spills,
flesh can be
peeled away
leaving the
image perfect.

Dionysus Abandons His Children at the First Promise of Skin Falling Upon Other Skin

Flesh is anchor,
is paradox, see:

    brushstroke, see

also: canvas. Flesh
is ugly ornament.

The Face of the Closest Woman to Zeus is the Face of Every Woman to Zeus

Blank slate
is full-throated

division sign
separating

birds from sky
leaving egg

as inexact
remainder.

John Clayton

Good Luck Bad Luck

Chopper noises are all around
Stretchers sitting on the ground
Blood seeping into the dirt
But Jim Bo Krenshaw does not hurt

It has been a real hard day
Pain and death is what we pay
going back to base camp now
with only sadness on our brow

Sitting on empty ammo cases
not thinking about safer places
Don't bogart that joint my friend
pass it over here again

Hot, wet, dirty and tired
we lost a little soul each time we fired
Hollowed eyes, exhausted faces
Dink ears on boot laces

Not for ideals, not for home
hoping to avoid a cold tombstone
Not for God or apple pie
just trying not to die

102 days of luck to go
247 days of luck to go
173 days of luck to go
He ran out of luck, Ole Jim Bo.

My Sister

He stood on a pile of rock
As we rolled into Pleiku.
He danced around like a fighting cock.

Hey, GI. My sista fuck you.
My sista, 5 dolla, GI.
You little bastard, bo di.

He was 10 and looked 6.
Dirty, hungry, and skinny as a stick.
He was barefoot, a booney hat on his head.

Hey, GI. My sista gotta bed.
You little Gook, are your ears full of shit.
Didn't you hear me when I said git!

He was desperate and could not go,
even if it meant pissing off Joe.

Get this convey to moving, man.
This kid is more than I can stand.

Come on, GI, my sista, 3 dolla, GI.
He said with a tear in his eye.

Bo di, bo di, bo di.
God damnit kid, do you want to die?
We're going to hell. We're going to fry.

My sista, 2 dolla, GI.

I thought to myself as we went on our way.
Shit, I'll never forget this hateful day.

The Box

I had to put you in a box.
To which only I can have a key.
I had to put you in a box,
So I am the only one who can see.

It was necessary you know.
I had to come back to the world,
And into society go.
No one could see the pain and anguish that in my heart
  swirled.

When your fate was found.
Near Mang Yang Pass in II Core,
By a single mortar round.
They took your life Jack, and never knew they even made
  a score.
That box is in my heart, where only I can see.
When I am alone, I put it in the lock
And then I turn the key,
And out you come with the other memories.

We can visit and talk and shoot the breeze and then it is
  time to go.
We have to keep it secret Jack, no one else must know.
That little trick keeps me safe from what we did so many
  years ago.

That stuff would make my family afraid, you know.
Jack, it's time to get back in the box.
What do you mean you're not ready to go?
Damn it, Jack, get back in the box.
You know I have to go.

Bottle on Fence Post by John E. Epic

Michael Joseph Arcangelini

Sleeping with Fireflies

Lightning bugs won't bite you,
nor do they sting,
nor do they crawl around
on your arm when you're
trying to eat a hot dog fresh
off a stick held over a roaring fire.
They do not dive bomb your ear, and
they don't go all kamikaze in your soda.

They just fly around in their own
little self-determined patterns
flirting with each other in
firefly semaphore,
bestowing magic on the muggy darkness,
meaning no one any harm
and no one means them any harm.

Even the children, who naively
capture them in peanut butter jars
washed out for just this purpose
with holes punched in the lid
and freshly pulled grass in the bottom,
mean them no harm. They are simply
enthralled with the wonder

of bioluminescence during twilight,
of the firefly in the summer night,
and they want to hold onto it,
set it next to their beds when
it is time to sleep, a nightlight,
a talisman, a way to bring magic
into the house, into their dreams.

A Slow Collapse

As though hesitant to
lie down at last
the old garage leans
precariously to the south
holding still in mid-collapse
occasionally shedding asphalt
shingles like lizard scales
like blue jay feathers lying
on the overgrown grass

an early morning fog
covers the old garage
like a pale ink wash
over a careful sketch
obscuring the details while
thickening the mood

the door hangs open,
a gaping, puzzled mouth,
I left it that way yesterday
when I decided I'd mown
enough yard for one day
and simply stopped, leaving
the mower where it sat and
the garage open to invasion by
all manner of nocturnal critters
rummaging about its contents

not caring that it leans
and one day will crash to
the ground in slow motion
lying still at last waiting to
be absorbed into the earth
sinking beneath the surface
and held there to become coal,
diamond, petrified wood
easing back up through the dirt
toward the surface and sunlight
a millennium from now.

Marcus Considers a Dog

A fairly large one, he thinks,
indolent by nature, stationary.
Not some miniature breed
bouncing off the walls,
needing constant attention,
yapping, yapping, yapping.

And not one always wanting to chase balls,
digging up the small yard,
tracking in mud,
barking at birds,
howling with distant sirens,
chewing up shoes,
needing to be constantly petted and fed.
Not that kind of attention sucking
black hole of a dog at all.

And not a St. Bernard, Sheepdog, or Samoyed
it must be one that doesn't shed
or need to be barbered and bathed too often;
nothing requiring frequent elaborate grooming.

And nothing that stares at him when he eats,
drooling from a droopy, pathetic face.
Not one that begs at all.

He wants one that blends into his environment
there, but out of the way until called on for
comfort, conversation, companionship;
grateful for food and a place to live.
A contented creature, self-contained,
happy to spend time by himself until
called on to be man's best friend.
That's the kind of dog Marcus wants.
He is open to suggestions.

Hunter Pender

This is one of many times I have written
about you

and you will taunt any dependency until you find out that
you have become one and then you become silent.

I have counted all of the moments when you are silent.

Counted the amount of coffee it takes me to lose focus.

The brain of an addict says yes and the body says yes and I
kept saying no and no until you threw your heart out into
the waves with no intent of breathing.

You drown like god like judas like a rosary in a war.

I break like porcelain like everything is still searching for you.

This midnight moon I force out of my mouth like a prayer.
This want of sanctuary.

Perhaps I will kiss all of our suicides back to where they
belong.

Kiss
my hands and spill the coffee.

You disassemble parts of you and I am still an addict with pomegranate breath.

Trying to get you to stay at least for winter.

At least until you say anything out of
your

heavy breathing
too distant
star colored mouth.

I am sitting alone with a cold cup of coffee

My body is half bent over itself and black circles are ringing around my eyes.
I am not thirsty or tired.
I am aching with heat.
I am aching with thoughts of your fingertips.

The kitchen is a silent space.
It is a room with smooth edges and a mosaic film of light.
Everything speaks softly.
Everything speaks with a whisper of dim on its tongue.
Every shade here is flowing and gentle.
The soft hues fit snuggly into my palms.
And I am static against the cotton morning.
harsh,
dark,
jagged.

I am finding sores and cramps in odd places: places outside of my body.
There are rashes and tenderness and little nerves that are exposed in more than just my teeth.
Everything hurts.
Even when it doesn't.

The cold coffee creaks down my throat and my head is boiling.

I pour everything down the drain in the sink and watch it choke out of my sight.
I try very hard to feel like I was not committing a small act of cannibalism.
The drinking of a blackness my nerves had run away to.

This is a seasick way. This almost but never quiet enough. This almost touching.

Dreams of cemented skies

// chandeliers crashing// spectrums colliding// rust bleeding into safe-waters// no man's land crumbling// the taste of freedom ripped out of my throat

Dreams of you speaking to me in a tongue I'd long since buried// remembrance of a veil that I placed upon it myself// fist digging into mouth// fingers trying to scrape out the rot// waking// mouth leaking ether of the graveyard my throat carries.

Dreams of ship stilling// drowning// keeping// waiting endless// time slowing// slower// faster// faster.

Dreams of bloodhounds chasing my dead// fangs clamping into phantom limbs// internal hemorrhaging// the grinding of marrow// leaking// spilling// of mouths howling echoes of distance.

Dreams of sutures ripped from wounds.

Dreams of butterflies feasting on the blood of yesterday.

You and I// I and You// Us – no longer// I.

Dreams of writing to you// coating each sentence in saliva that promises to translate// burying every word in the gaps between my teeth// waking to a tongue that cannot.

Dreams of another lifetime// one where I kept the faith// do you remember?

Paperweight dreams anchor us to the other.

Jane McElroy Butler

Autumnal Devotions

A tree stands lanky and lovely.
It becomes the first to paint the sky.
Peachy and bright, it shrugs itself into autumn.
Brown leaves descend.
Children run through the crunch...crunch
of the newly, dearly departed.

A tree clutches itself, drawing close its branches.
It makes one final shiver.
The tiniest of leaves falls to the earth below,
adding to the heart of beautiful harvest hues.

Searching

I find poems to write
in the words that settle
to the ground
when you leave.

Walking around all day,
kicking up words
that lie deep
in the carpet:

a jumble of vocabulary
that even the vacuum cannot
suck up with its loud,
whirring sound.

I wait for the words
to settle, then gently
pick them up--
one at a time--

each word loaded
with double meanings;
and still I write on
through the day:

I am balance,
I am calm,
I am peace,
I am calm.

I am searching for you.
Where have you gone?
You are settled into
words on the carpet,
as well, hiding.

The Storm

A pink and yellow shower of mountain roses rains down before me

as distant hailstones glance off the rocks of Mount Lemon.

Hanging wisteria moves gently in the quiet breeze of the oncoming storm.

Light rain drips from the bees nest; a cicada shell blows by

(it sang itself entirely away).

Morning Glory and Bush Clover bend over as if to worship

the drizzle held so tenderly in their buds.

Heat waves that shimmered one or two inches above the rocks

are now washed away in absolution.

A caterpillar, even this late in autumn, catches my eye--

She will never become a butterfly.

But as the rain stops, the moon flowers.

Tractors and Chevy by John E. Epic

Michael Hackney

Amazing & Delicious

Amazing & delicious
to write when the music
pierces the heart this way.
These Van Morrison songs
are so ambrosial, they
must have a special
place for him in heaven.
I play the fool
by comparison & offer
a simple fugue; I feed
on absinthe & the lore
of false gods.

But this is all that I am:
dust & a little oil, my poetry
abstract & hard to know.
What is laid bare is negotiable

& poems are often scrappy.

Cincinnati

I put a little
whip cream on you
and eat you all up
at the school dance,
Molly Ringwald.
And, well,
you don't kiss me.
You don't give
any indication
that you even like
Bruce Springsteen
albums.

I just play
in the arcade,
watch the shake
of your head,
the shape
of your hips.

Don't leave me
in Cincinnati
with a bag
of scones
staring at
the hotel bill.
Down escalator…
Would rather be
up skirt.

The Problem

The problem is,
we think we have time.
Time enough to describe
the swath of butterflies
hovering just below
our knees this morning.
out by the railroad tracks,
you and I lighting up
our cigarettes.
The quickening pace
of life leads us not
to pick mulberries,
leisurely, in the yard,
but inside to coffee-shop
air-conditioning
to talk of coast-to-coast
motorcycle trips never taken
and novels never written.
Outside, in summer rain,
newly-minted raindrops
turn to steam as they hit
pavement.

Did you notice?

Kerry Trautman

The Sound of Your Own Voice

How does one Tern or Wren discern a friend's call when
I turn every time I hear *Mom!* called across a crowd?

Each bird's warbling squeaks and chits too similar
whether Lesser Tit or Greater, whether Pitpit or Plover.

In high school there were girls I wanted to be friends with
though I didn't know much about them.

A friend tells me I *write about birds a lot*.
And I do, though they're basically strangers.

There are birds I recognize by body or sound,
but few I know by both. I want to befriend them.

If someone calls *Terry* or *Karen* I will whip
my head, searching for who might need me.

Would I know a Blackbird if it was night?
In daylight would I assume a Meadowlark?

I have one of those faces that looks like other people's.
I am one of those bodies easily forgotten.

Turning my ear toward birdsong doesn't always reveal
a body. A watched beak doesn't always sing on cue.

Who are you, I hear? A Hedge Sparrow, House Sparrow,
or, if it's dusk or night, a Pipistrelle?

A friend says it's ok that I hate the sound of my own voice,
says she hates hers too, says no one really hears theirs right.

Am I to blame for turning toward what I think is my name,
shooting awake having heard it, ears cottoned full of hope?

Wisdom

(after a mixed media painting by Randy Bennet)

St. Apollonia[1],
my daughter's jaw needs your wisdom
this morning, four teeth jerked away
as crows cawed outside
the oral surgeon's window.

Things will be taken from her
over and over again.
There aren't feathers enough to
embellish this knowledge.

St. Thomas Aquinas[2],
our schoolchildren need your robes
to shield them at their desks.
Buzzards soar above their jungle gyms,
sniffing for gunpowder.

There are always talons poised to uproot
tender feet from soil.

St. Luke the Evangelical[3],
take Apollonia's hand,
deflect the light, so my girl
cannot walk toward it.

Assure her there is nothing there to see.
That her regular Friday is worth finishing.

My daughter's physics teacher drew
diagrams of birds' wings and loft,
of levers and wedges and
the arcs of projectiles.

St. Gabriel Possenti4,
lower any barrels raised at living targets,
intercede between flesh and lead,
alter trajectories.

Greyblack shadows hover circles over
calculus class and biology and
a Tuesday morning ACT administration.

Second-grade teachers are skilled at
pulling baby teeth.
Older, we dream our teeth fall out,
wake to dried drool on our cheek,
licking the rows to check
they're each accounted-for.

St. Dymphna5,
relax troubled psyches.
Numb triggers and their fingers.

My girl will rest the weekend away
with pain pills, ice cream, and tv.

St. Raphael6,
you're overwhelmed.
Beg the aid of blue-jays and goldfinches
like Sleeping Beauty might.
Make prisms from what pinpoints
of light you find in our dark.

Roasting Turkey for Friends

Drippings crackle brown to the roasting pan
and the house is gauzed with rosemary smoke.
The beast's neck and gizzards poach in celery,
sage and an onion's outermost white cloak.
Outside, January bombasts itself
against the windows and kowtow-ing shrubs.
As a girl I would wake Thanksgiving late
morning at my grandparents' quiet house
to the same sizzle, bake and boil, to the
oiled mechanisms of seasonal feast,
the small bathroom, with its ever-closed door,
the only room in the house left unsmoked
and cool with fogged window and sweet soap—like
stepping into a cardinal's startled heart.

Daniel Crocker

How Me and Lord Byron Got our Grooves Back

I'm having beers
with Warren Zevon
We're talking
about our cancers

It's boring
I may not even have
cancer
Warren certainly doesn't

He wants
to invite Kerouac
but I'm tired
and Kerouac
cries into his whiskey
and it always ends when he
demands to be draped in
an American Flag and buried
up north

I was tired of everything
at that point
in the deep south
so many miles from my wife
and Adrienne Rich rebuffing
my every advance

Let me show you how it's done
Byron says
I don't know where he came
from but his entrance a
dramatic flapping of a cape
was something to behold

What else can I do
I sit back and watch
It's impressive. You'd think
him a young David Lee Roth
In the end, however,
It doesn't go any better
for him that it did me

Tonight, Adrienne says
no poetry will serve
and that seems to be the gist
of the whole goddamned thing

All of us brooding on the mistakes
we just can't seem to write our way
out of
those long haul problems
stretch out like the Mississippi
waters the deep troubled waters
the anxieties of speaking

The things hidden so well
no one can fault you for them
clasped so tightly no one would
bother to steal them and even if
they did what could they do

We find some joy in that
and a few other things
and think maybe we should
invite old Jack over after all

He may have cried, just a little
trying to compare Byron's cape
to the spasm of a dying catfish
He never did get
that image just right
but Jesus Christ
his hair was

C is for Cookie

I won't believe this is real
anymore. Like I'm going to just
lay here all night shaking, thinking again
of the cookie when there is a jar full
in the kitchen and if those are gone
a gas station just down the road

It's hard. My father loved the Oreo
and his father the macaroon. It was
good enough for them, I thought,
it's good enough for me

But cookies are what got me into this
mess, cookies are why I quiver,
but I'd known only hunger when
the chickens from my cookie eating
days finally came home to roost

The things I did all hopped up
on cookies do not suffer forgiveness
I've been a bad monster. In my endless
thirst maybe

I wasn't thinking straight. Maybe
she'd just given me all the forgiveness
she had to give. Maybe it didn't matter
that I had given up cookies

because I still thought of them. I still
kept one in my desk drawer just in case
You don't have to talk when you've got
a fig newton in your mouth. There's no
room to think with a mind full of sugar

So when she asked
I cracked one wide
and a million different
fortunes spread before us
I opened my mouth to
say so but it hung
a gaping black wound

all my life I've known silence
except deep down
where it whispers
insistently
madly
finally
Cookie
Cookie
Cookie!

Mania Makes Me A Better Poet

I paced up and down the front porch on a rare, cool Missouri night.

"The government wants me to take pills," I told my wife. She asked why, but I didn't have an answer. Part of me knew it wasn't true. Part of me wasn't convinced. My thoughts shifted rapidly.

"Do you ever wonder about that guy from the Oak Ridge Boys? You know, the one with the big beard?" I had also suddenly become obsessed by William Lee Golden. I was worried about him.

"Do you think he feels trapped? Like, he wishes he could shave off that scraggly damned beard and be free of it?"

I wondered if he'd ever regretted growing that beard, probably sometime in his early twenties, and regretted it.

"He has to think his fans just won't get the real Oak Ridge Boys experience without it? And what about John Berryman? Did he have the same problem? Is that why he jumped off that bridge?"

This was just a few days before I broke down, went to a clinic, and got help for bipolar 1 disorder. The symptoms had been ramping up for months—compulsive intrusive thoughts and rituals—*I'm going to kill myself tomorrow* was a favorite of mine, running on a loop in my mind. I was trucking along on little to no sleep or food. My speech was pressured. The mania had started out fun. I was creative. I felt unstoppable. I had the energy to do some work. In the end it always gets scary. It devolves into anxiety, paranoia and the occasional mild delusion.

In the end, however, I got a hell of a poem about William Lee Golden out of it.

The truth is, mania makes me a better poet, although it's taboo to say so. Not among other bipolar people. We'll readily admit to each other that we love parts of our mania. We usually just don't tell the sane people in our lives. They look at us shocked, or sad, or worse. Sometimes they look at us with anger. Our loved ones have seen the wake of destruction left behind by mania. I've hurt plenty of people myself while manic, including my significant other. I swear by my medications now. They keep me stable, if not fully content. Sometimes something is missing.

Unless you've been through it, you just can't understand how mania feels. It's like being on speed and booze at the same time—except better. Your mind, at least for a while, is laser-focused. You actually have the desire and energy to want to create—or do whatever it is that you do. Depression, on the other hand, is a creativity killer. It can be hard to get out of bed, much less write a poem. Mania, when it hits just right, calls for hours of steady work.

This is the hypomania stage—which is where mania ends for many bipolar people. For me, however, it goes further than that. I eventually sink into paranoia, anxiety and, yes, on a few occasions, delusions. This is the difference between bipolar 1 and 2. Bipolar 2 experience hypomania. If you've had even one delusional mania, you are probably bipolar 1. Of course, it's much more complicated than that, but for the sake of this essay that's all you really need to know. So, I guess it's really this little band of, with apologies to astrophysicists, the Goldilocks zone that I love.

Still, we must not admit it. It makes sane people mad if you tell them that mania is fun, or that you miss it so much you might even go off of your medication for a while.

Nothing worries my wife more than me going into a mania. When it does happen, she usually notices before I do. It's the fast-talking, I think. Or it's the constant work. The first thing she usually says to me, and it's wise, "Don't make any major decisions without asking me first." I don't want to lump all bipolar people into one group. It's a very complex disease that treats people differently. Many bipolar folks hate their mania in every stage. I'm just not one of them.

It's like there's only aspect of mania, or mental illness in general, we can talk about and that's the downside. The chaos left in its wake. The ashes left behind from the fire. As a friend of mine put it, they don't want us to feel good. They want us to feel normal. But we're not normal and normal for us feels blank and boring and depressing and flat. We've touched a bit of magic that lays beyond that. Some people call it crazy.

I'm here to write about the upside of mania though. Is it worth it? Maybe. I guess that depends on how much you love whatever poetry is for you. Psychiatrists will tell us that this desire to be in touch, be a part of, mania again is just part of the disease. That we need to fight it and do everything we can to remain stable. But sometimes we'll risk everything just to taste it again. We'll take a medication vacation. We'll do things that trigger mania in us on purpose in hopes that it works. Of course, by "we" I don't mean every bipolar person. I don't even mean every bipolar creative person. But, I have talked to enough to know, and have had conversations on online support group enough times that I can say with some confidence that it's a big part of us.

But, here I am doing everything I can to be as normal as I can. I've been stable on my medication for over a year now, except for one minor mania, and I also haven't written a poem worth a real shit. I've written some okay to pretty good poems, but the best poems I've ever written are all tinged with at least a little mania. (Many of you out there might argue that I've never written a good poem either way). I guess, in full disclosure, I should say that I'm in a slight mania right now, and I decided to stop my medications for a few days hoping for it to ramp up just a little more. I'm in a safe place (a writer's retreat) where I can risk it. That statement alone will probably have this essay dismissed by a large chunk of readers, but I'm not writing this essay for normal people. I'm writing it for people like me.

    Sometimes the chaos is worth it. Sometimes I'm in love with chaos. That said, I'm not advocating for anyone to stop taking their medications. It's not good for you. It's not healthy. But, I know many of us still do it. It might even be irresponsible for me to write about the good parts of mania. While it's different for everyone, however, it's there. I've talked to a wide variety of bipolar people while writing this essay, and they mostly agree. Mania is great. Until it's not.

    I take my medication because of the hurt I've caused in the past. Because I've lost my mind in the past. Because they make me a worse poet, but a better person. Mostly I take them for people I love. Not for me. I like the way my mind works off of them. So sometimes, a little medication vacation is in order. It's been three days. I felt mania coming on, a slight one, and wanted to see where it goes. It's 2am. I just finished up a poem, smoked my last cigarette of the night, and typed these final lines looking out onto the empty streets of Belle, Missouri. Just me and my old friend. I'll start taking my medications again tomorrow.

Portrait of Jason Ware by John E. Epic

Paul Koniecki

Because It Has
No Natural Enemies

The clouds are a body at rest.
Near dark
arrows and bolts fall to the bottom
of the creek.
Some things are safe
to reflect in or against.
Our markers
are bits
of broken branch and smaller
twigs.
As we run through the trees
in a zig-zag of dodge bark
the lakes and the sky are mirrors set
at angles to mirrors.

Tonight we are going to The Fair
for salt-water taffy pulled
one thousand times
the return of the big
wheel
ransom washed down with cold
thick root beer and ice
cream floats we call brown cows.

Tomorrow
when there is no more forest for the trees
we will go to the roof and shout
to all the gods in heaven.

Why is our love so large?
Because it has no natural enemies.

The Dells - July 1976

it's a beautiful night i'm running home
spinning around tree roots and sidewalk cracks
like a pinwheel on a carousel

———————

Baskets of fish
fell across the
lawn like hail

between buildings and
homes,

a gift for
the lost cats, the orphans,
and the misers

from our Lord.
The strays feasted

and I fried my share.
No prediction and

no report of
this in the news,
too Christlike to have risen
circulation,

weather again threatening to reach
beyond commercial regard.

Too Late to Miss the Brewery Work

Imago, in this daydream all the parents
have antlers and they are surrounded
by oak trees or pine. Sap, needles, bark

like dry and peeling hide, too thin
branches, if I'm wrong about the pine
I'm right about the oak. We needed

somewhere smooth to carve our names
or nail real two-by-four steps up to forts
in waiting. Willows to swing. Crabapples

to throw. Good bole knots to hide bad magazines.
Spitting pinched chaw like
worm dirt in shit-colored streams from

want to be fisherman's tongues. Breaking
the Earth with our saliva we asked when does the rain come?
Scientists count

three billion trees and less than we used
to be. Now the smell of yeast is only for the tour. Still young,
our piss is for ourselves.

R.C. Patterson

What Does It Mean to be a Realist?

What does it mean to be a realist?
It means that happiness exists.
Happiness is as real as numbers drifting like fall
foliage creating a collage painting the canvas of my
imagination, because I see love in the faces of people
who fly through life like biplanes.
Nothing is more beautiful than a positive attitude.
An attitude as genuine as my niece when she says

I love you uncle, look what I got you for your birthday.

As she holds a notebook with several strips of paper
haphazardly glued to the cover.
I refuse to tell her that it's not my birthday.
But this is that honesty that I seek to be like.
Honesty is also real.
Love is real.
This is what it means to be a realist.

Elegy 1 of Erotica Matrix

Here's where I have planted my garden
whose golden fruits are products of
noumenal experiences in the fifth
dimension. A damsel with dementia
weeps parabolas bleeding from
Polonius, stabbed with polonium
Spears.
Apollo must be balanced!
This is why I left the Matrix
with Morpheus.
The Dionysian
machine rivers wake me up from hypnosis.

Trees are pikes impaling
the earth draining her,
like leeches on a lake of blood.
Clouds are gray canvases
I painted with my eyes.
I painted the green,
but it's winter
The damsel with dementia
followed me.
Now I feel my two-ness.
Split like a pizza.
Dinner for Apollo
and the Dionysian.

Trapped Like Mice

Trapped like mice in high towers.
Invisible red lines keep me from food.
He keeps me from her.
Kept from bread crumbs.
Cut off from love.

Trapped like mice in high towers.
Just waiting to starve, to end this living.
Cut off from friends.
No company in this prison.
Just waiting to starve, alone, so hungry.
Why am I still trapped, you won, you don't need me!

Trapped like mice in high towers.
Red lines get trampled.
Burned up and shattered.
Pushed to revolt, can't keep us from shit.
Pushed to assault these red lines and gatekeepers.
I am free, you lost, I can finally see her!

But she found me beneath the rubble of towers.
Cut off from love, her love grew sour.
Kept from bread crumbs.
Her children starved trapped like mice in high towers.

John Dorsey

Passing Through Leadwood
for Daniel Crocker

just off the ferlin husky highway
i think what would richard hugo
say about this town
that you haven't screamed
in your sleep
a thousand times before

fueled by wonder bread & poison
sad songs about tradition & empty storefronts
the ghosts that go away quietly
because they know
that they won't be missed

the buildings that crumble
& just slip away
from their foundations

the houses that look normal
the regret that is bought
& paid for
in generations of blood

where the sky is a rusted satellite dish
a dirty diaper on the sidewalk
next to the high school

you & icarus are famous here
like ferlin husky on the wings of a dove

traveling through the body like cancer

on its way to somewhere else

some far away land

where there is nothing to do
but sing.

Rosalea Ain't Dead Yet
for Victor Clevenger & Michael Hathaway

in front of the st. john courthouse annex
we notice a bumper sticker
on the back of a minivan

rosalea ain't dead yet

she stands there in tears
punching numbers into the sun
like a holocaust survivor
she once met here as a girl

like a ghost
like a relic
like a tumbleweed
like a bomb
going off
in her heart

like a religion
like a miracle

while in harper kansas
they plaster posters on trees
plant nooses around the necks of sunflowers

red tulips are painted gray
glass blown out of the windows

in front of her hotel
in front the old anchor oyster parlor

black birds & gas station girls
ask if we are famous
& rosalea pulls a blanket over her head
to keep out the moonlight

the prairie connection

nothing is sacred here
but time

& rosalea ain't dead yet

and the red sea
was once a wheat field
a burning building
meant to raise the dead

& rosalea ain't dead yet

she ain't dead yet

until the prairie
comes & takes
her very last breath

takes her tongue
takes everything

that hasn't somehow
already blown away.

A Ghost is an Unforgiving River

at forty-one
i've learned that we're only as fast
as what we can outrun

that my legs were rubber bands
in another life
the product of a war
i'll never win

a foreign body of water
an unforgiving river

memories only immigrate
to other parts of the brain

other borders of the heart
that never close

blood rarely changes course

rarely does the right thing

when you expect it to.

Harmonize by Joel Lipman

Jackie Magnuson Ash

Season's End

What happened was this: After her dad finished
unloading the final load of milo, he shut off the
combine's engine, climbed out to sit on its metal
landing, closed his eyes, and there they waited for
him—sister, dad, Uncle Louie, floating against
darkness, standing in the order of their deaths.
His booted feet rested on a ladder rung, hands
going slack in his lap, head leaning against the
railing, his soiled felt hat tipped off center. From
the foot of the ladder, her mom called his name.
An October breeze lifted fodder into the air.
She called again. After a third time—it was more of a
shout—he awoke. Climbing down the ladder, he said
nothing of the vision, not then. For the next week he
went on with end-of-season chores. Just after sunup
one morning, he couldn't get out of bed, couldn't
move at all. An ambulance sirened him into town.

He's frail now, an old man at 63.

Makeshift

The tin-skirted house, doublewide,
well-used, glinty in the sun, now sits
in a brome field across the creek.
On this clean-skied day she kneels
at the edge of plowed ground to take
a picture, not of the makeshift house
but of the landscape. Her boy darts
into the field, onto turned earth
and faces the camera square,
hair the color of sunshine. Her girl,
toddler plump, halts on uneven clods,
frowns, wants to be where her brother is.

The co-op elevator pins the distance.
It's the only village stake. The tiny church
burned years ago. Nellie's store has closed.

Nellie said to her mother yesterday,
I see your daughter hung her curtains.
The trailer is now officially a home.

In the field her children wait, obedient,
watch her snap the shutter, draw them in.

First Fall

The smell of fuel and oil permeates the air. Just beneath it, a hint of fresh earth. From the open-air seat of the idling tractor, he gazes at the field, the last one planted. He drilled the wheat as straight as he could, taking care to keep sight of his mark at the end of the first pass, just as his father-in-law taught him.

He reaches for the gearshift, foot pressing down on the clutch, but stops mid motion. A fox has darted out from trees along the road. It angles across the field toward the river. As it gets closer, he sees a tinge of red on its gray fur, sees also a neon green tennis ball in its mouth. What dog did it steal that from? Don't the Plains Indians call the fox the Trickster, or is that just the coyote? Is this an omen? He laughs at himself. The fox runs on past, ignoring the tractor, and disappears over a rise in the ground.

In the direction of home, sky above yellowing cottonwoods has deepened into a blue-violet promise of rain. Seed is in the ground, and next June will bring his harvest.

John Macker

Border Wall Blues

When not speaking in tongues
its soullessness borders on the devout.
From the top of the wall, we're out of range
of anything animated or proselytizing
from the top of the wall
there are no degrees of separation
from the heat
the desert is a fever dreamt graveyard and
the wind is alive with hymns.
The wall wages a war of insurrection
on the landscape
dispossessed javelina mothers cry at the moon
rattlesnakes sell death rattles
safe for children without homes.

From up here, *el norte* loses its cool
but you can watch Jesus cross the Rio Grande
his flotation device a crown of thorns.
Mourning wolves' claws are styluses at play
in the furrows of the earth
evolution will one day take their sight
because of the impenetrable sameness of the night.

El linea is a lit fuse blessed by Saint Anthony
red dirt (marijuana) knocks on the door
of wall and is asked for its credentials
the view from the wall is *commensurate with*
 my capacity for wonder.

From the top of the wall
a couple of gringo poets under the spell
of some ebullient *anejo,*
talk surfing, confederate generals and
their capacity for wonder borders on the devout.
From the top of the wall you can see Zapata's horse
ride into the tequila sunrise and
pose for Diego Rivera's mural
while the sky shelters its rainbows from the dull light of day.
Wall's famous shadow is a military asset, is
impetuous and waits for nobody.

You can watch the children play cat's cradle
in the arroyo bottoms and learn to flirt
with the paranoia of barbed wire.

You can fill this hollow wall with the blues,
narcocorridos, the deported, the disappeared
our confederate generals
the bones of turkey vultures
splinters of our national cartilage
this is how we give solace to the underworld.

From here the crossers can see America's rapacious
crumbling beauty. Its army of oxidized statuary
in the moodiest of public parks reimagines war.
From the top of the wall the winds
drift down to Mexico and emboldened heat
they blow the untrammeled dust of crossers
until they've extinguished all fires.
This part of the wall is hell bent for heaven
because heaven invented speaking in tongues.
This part of the wall is dedicated to wooly
mammoths who once claimed all of Aztlán
as home, who respected no borders, whose
ghost migrations still leave deep tracks.
To the Rufous hummers who've been around as
long as the jawbone of an ass, who spend
twenty percent of their waking moments
in combat, who fly south every year
and obey the instinct that says one day
this ground will be made whole.

From the top of your lungs you can sing
              the partially eclipsed, white nationalist
                            grindhouse grievous angel blues.

Empty Foxhole

Ornette Coleman's death is the shape
of deaths to come. He played the
breathless language of improvisational
blues and jazz until I could feel the world
embrace his overheated romantic madness.
It filled every foxhole with uninterrupted prayer.
Listening to Ornette I felt his sacred heart
blues, his squash blossom blues, his darkened
street blues. Listening to Ornette, he could rub his hands
together like a shaman's and create sparks.
Listening to Ornette is to hush the earth
blazing with war songs. Listening to Ornette
the summer heat seeks my bones
disappeared cities no longer spark the horizon.
His, the soul end of endings, the
lone gunman of ecstatic blow.

Buried Poem
After Sam Shepard

The last motel room standing
with its million neon eyes
mad drunks and samurai crucifixions
died last night in Barstow
and Truth or Consequences, or Baggs, Wyoming

Where we tore each other up in the dark and
reassembled ourselves, there were words for that.

There were words for the silences
and inflamed heirlooms, the migrations
our fathers left us –
endless abandoned blue streaks
of "that was the whisky talking" until the words
dried up emptied of all but their machismo.

There were words for motels like morose
wickiups where the past tongue-lashed
memory for failure to forgive after
all these years.

Room service stalked you
across the desert like a serial killer!
We watched you in that Cold in July flick,
Your character as taciturn as a tombstone.

What dystopia in human form
looked like ground to a pulp.

You made us famous for our trespasses,
our outlaw mouths,
our incendiary family arrhythmias.
There were words for every cutthroat summer
for every middle distance
as American as wide open space that disappears
while a river cleaves its fatally untamed ground.

Maryfrances Wagner

The Immigrants Get a New Camera

No one knew when they stood on Stanley Hill,
each waiting to hold the new family camera.
They didn't mind sharing among the eleven of them,
one capturing the bridge over the north end, another
the city skyline, the old airport. Sadie took candids
of Josie scratching her bites, Lena hiking up her
sagging skirt. Sam lined up Gene and Phil saluting,
Jay making a pig face, Nene showing his new tooth
coming in, all of them in costumes they'd found
at the dump. It was all about holding the black box
for the first time, framing those frozen moments
before listening for the lever's click. Frank snapped
Rosie singing *The Continental* while she swished
the yellow skirt of her dance hall costume,
little Martha imitating her sister's swing,
Nene turning somersaults down the hill.
No one knew they couldn't afford film.

Demoni

Demons haunted the house
on Camel Street, made Papa
drop his fork, wave his shotgun.
The children huddled under the table.

One Christmas, *demoni*
let a pig in to root through
wrapped yo-yos and knitted sweaters.
Shivering under blankets,
Sadie and Lena heard them
on the steps, heard glass
hit the fireplace.
Basta, Nonna said. *No more
trees, no wrapped presenti.
Now on, peanuts and oranges.*

The next fall, Martha asked nightly
for a doll. *No store bambola,*
Papa said and whittled her a horse.
Rosie sharpened a pencil,
wrote Tom Pendergast:
*If you care so much
about the poveri, then
buy my sister a doll.*

On Christmas Eve, the *bambola*
arrived in silver paper.
Papa set down his carved sheep,
his crate of oranges.
Nonna crossed herself,
whispered, *Demoni.*
Rosie and Martha twirled,
then sharpened another pencil.

Zia Rosie Talks About the Family Farm

We never knew we were poor. Always plenty to eat. Had two cows named Bay and Rosie. We used to squirt each other with the milk. Your father and Jay pulled a calf out of Rosie's stomach once. Martha and I scooted around to watch behind the fence. The calf came out the wrong way. It was already dead, and the cow was in so much pain. It kept ooooohhhh hing. Nonna made ricotta and mozzarella with the milk. We had goats too, and sometimes Papa killed a goat. He'd get a stick to pull the skin off. After he killed it, he tied it up and plunged a dagger in its neck and prayed and prayed. The blood poured out into a bucket. He put the stick up through the foot and worked off the hide. The stick had a hole in it so he could blow air and make the skin swell. Then he could pull it off. If you didn't do it right, it ruined the meat. People always wanted to buy half a goat at Easter. Gina always said she didn't want to eat any goat, but at dinner, she always ate the most. Papa also sheared sheep, and your dad held the sheep down while Papa sheared them. Wool popped out all over. Nonna washed the fleece and stuffed the mattresses with it. It got knotty, but she'd pull it back apart and fluff it up. She made blankets out of the wool. Before he married Nonna, Papa herded sheep. They both wanted lots of children. Nonna was 44 when she had Aunt Martha, and if nothing had happened to Papa, they wanted even more. We think she had fifteen, and at least two died in Italy. A son named Diaspro and a girl named Rosa. Guess they wanted kids with those names because they used them again. We knew two died here, one an infant and one at three, and then we lost Frank in a car accident when he was eighteen. That left ten of us. Still a bunch of us sitting at the dinner table every night.

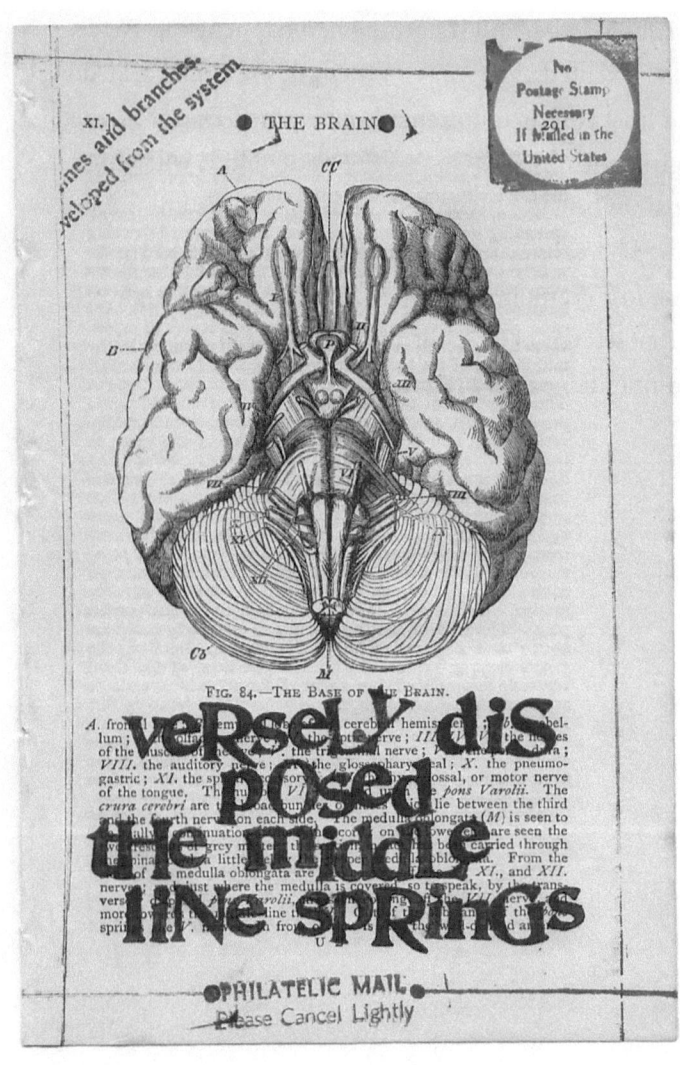

The Brain by Joel Lipman

Xanath Caraza

El huracán

Extendidas las hélices
alcanzas las palabras.

Torbellino de
agua y viento.

Fuerza arrasadora
cortas las sílabas,
te mezclas con las páginas.

Ancestral ira y desencanto.

Juntos en un solo instante
levantan el agua del mar,
llevan la fuerza de Chaac.

El aliento divino no deja
de traer la lluvia.

Los pelícanos
planean con el viento,
se montan en las olas.

El abismo acuático
despierta de su sueño
y con tan solo un respiro
hace temblar.

Destructora exhalación,
es amor lo que derrotará
al corazón, no la ira.

The Hurricane

With the helixes extended
you attain the words.

Whirlwind of
water and wind.

Devastating strength
you slice syllables,
intermingling with the pages.

Ancestral wrath and disillusion.

Together for a single instant
they raise the water from the sea,
wielding the strength of Chaac.

Divine breath continues
to bring the rain.

Pelicans
hover on the wind,
they ride the waves.

The aquatic abyss
awakens from its dream
and causes trembling
with a single breath.

Destructive exhalation,
it is love, not wrath,
that will vanquish the heart.

El mar se vuelve espejo

El mar se vuelve espejo
después de la tormenta.

Haces de luces doradas
y zafiros rayos hienden
el apaciguado sueño.

La noche engulle el color.

El viento recorre
la superficie de azogue
y lo pinta de olas.

Escarpadas pinceladas
en la cutícula acuática.

El viento y el color
transgreden
el manto lacustre

mientras en el horizonte
muere el sol de fuego.

Humo lunar reemplaza
la luz del crepúsculo.

Argenta líquida y obsidiana
en la memoria de agua.

The Sea Turns Mirror

The sea turns mirror
after the storm.

Shafts of golden luminosity
and sapphire light rend
the tranquil dream.

Night devours color.

The wind traverses
the quicksilver surface
and paints it with waves.

Strenuous brushstrokes
on the aquatic cuticle.

Wind and color
transgress
the lacustrine cloak

while the fiery sun
withers on the horizon.

Lunar smoke replaces
crepuscular light.

Liquid silver and obsidian
in the memory of water.

Oleaje

Oleaje, bate tus pesadas
aguas en mis peñascos.

Choca tus densas
corrientes en las arterias.

Crea un furioso mar
en las entrañas

antes de que todo
se desvanezca.

Sumérgete, luz dorada,
en el abismal recuerdo de ayer.

Waves

Waves, beat your weighty
waters upon my cliffs.

Crash your dense
currents in my arteries.

Create a furious sea
in my entrails

before everything
dissipates.

Immerse yourself, golden light,
in the vast memory of yesteryear.

George Wallace

HOW IT WILL END
City by city,
block by block,
in seed and in blood,
this symphony of eyes,
this christening of stars,
village to village,
heart to hand,
you who have taken over
and control too much,
you who have held us down
too long, we will speak out against
you, classroom by classroom, hall
by hall, no death threat can contain
us, no kidnapping silence, this song
we sing, kitchen by kitchen, room by room,
this contagion of the people, this bird which
wants to escape, which must escape, no cage of gold
can hold our discontent, no bullethole of mass distraction,
jail by jail, judge by judge, we will gather up and we will
overthrow you, no government propaganda machine can
shut us down, no fear brigade, no killing crew, no lie of lust
or vanity, and no, not flattery, nothing can stop us from gathering,

Revolution is a small boy reading whitman at a long
wooden table; revolution is a small girl carrying the
book of the world in secret hands; revolution is a young
woman and a young man making love against your terrible
red glare;

And a breeze blows freely through an open door,
and buttercups grow freely through cracked cement,
and we are those flowers and we are that breeze
and we shall not bear your oppression long, the people
we shall wake to our duty soon, the people!
free to stand against you
free to expose you —
snitches and bullies
cowards and thugs —
we shall laugh out loud or die,
we shall beat ten thousand holes
in your useless armor — tank and
troop commander, dictator and hench-
man, informer and border patrol —
and we shall live again, free!

In the precious light of the people's sun
which shines through.

DREAM CHILD ILLUMINATES HERSELF

Standing at the corner of 39th and Bell like a river that
flows up she wants to take off her zipcode bandana
and fling it like a flying saucer at the boys in Prospero's
picture window who are gawking at her in their
pheremone hats — none of them can dish like Betty or
beat dawn across the state line — she's too wise for this
shit but she digs the boy who speaks Chinese and went
to Sacramento to sit at the holy knee of Gary Snyder and
she would like to do that too, go to Sacramento, she'd like
to dance like a raincloud full of heaven right out of this
cow town and into The Zen

She is strong and present
nothing can hold her down

too low to the sky, too high for men

WATCH ME BURN IT TO THE GROUND IN THE TALLGRASS, BABY

This is how to bounce in the free world baby
tall in the tall grass this is how to live on the
edge this is how to put down the gun pick
up the groove and fear nothing, live on the
outside — this is how to walk the liberation
walk make a big ugly footprint in the lily
white snow —

This way next stop new existence, exit stage
right from the systematic FBI ass-fuck tent

Exit this way to the skyblue limit to the road
for eagles — exit this way, get out of the way,
meet me in the next century it looks like it's
going to get ugly around here because it is,
let's just keep passing thru, don't try to stop
us motherfuckers.

I do not care what your church of trump got to
say i do not care what your evangelical squeaky
clean russian hooker church of golden shower
hypocrisy got to say —

Take your redneck handshake take your wall
street three piece take your rich boy bodysuit
and frack it.

Take your filthy money and stick it back in your
pocket, what's money got to do with it — you
want to walk that way then go ahead but keep
your hands off a free man's groove —

And guess what if you build a wall it'll swallow
you up whole and leave you rotten and the rest
of the planet free, and if you want to know
the truth i know my enemy and it's you.

I ain't going to say nothing you say i ain't going to oblige.

Because no i am no problem child but i do not
subscribe no not to your fascism not to your greed
no not to your how-to who-to when-to what-to —

What did it ever get anyone in the end except headlines —

And who's gonna stop me? no not you mister
groovecop no not you mister talk show fox news
tv propaganda queen.

No not you mister swear on a stack of bibles
robot, mister right wing dope blind hashtag
chalkmark tweet-a-minute prison yard bigot.

Guard me all day long if you want to reverend
nobody — no one gonna tell me what.

Watch me burn it to the ground in the tallgrass. baby.

Chigger Matthews

(for people who laugh at death)

children at the table
next to mine
are singing

everybody dies!
everybody dies!

stabbing each other
in the ribs with
plastic spoons

laughing until tears
stream down their faces

bucketshovels at sundown
(or, where Murphy lay)
for Mark McClane

Murphy whom I called
the demon-dog Murphistopheles
and others called
Murph

had a mulch factory
and a river-stick retrieval service
paid in head pats and late night
varmint raids but now

now he is gone
                            gone
                                                gone

to wherever farm dogs go
when then they go
to the big farm
in the sky

Baron put down the last stick
and everyone said a few words

Hot dog said the gravedigger
waving away the flies

Tempus fugit said the flies
but no one was in the mood
for jokes

Good boy said we all
as the master laid him down

I poured out my drink
laid some flowers on the dirt
and let the old boy
learn a new trick

To Ronnie with Love
for Mark Shaffer

You were buried
at home in Elysium
when your last lover
put your ashes in the ground
by the dog bones
under the cherry tree.

At your ceremony
well attended by ruby throated Aztec warriors
the ghosts of Roman soldiers
and whatever family is left.

The Emperor sings,
all we ask is instant death
and the Chorus refrains,
give it to us or we'll take it!

Then we danced for your safe return
ate smoking bar-be-que
and after El Pastor left
hit a joint
in memory.

You would have wanted it that way.

*Elysium is the Roman analog of Edenic paradise; Aztec warriors were believed to reincarnate as hummingbirds.

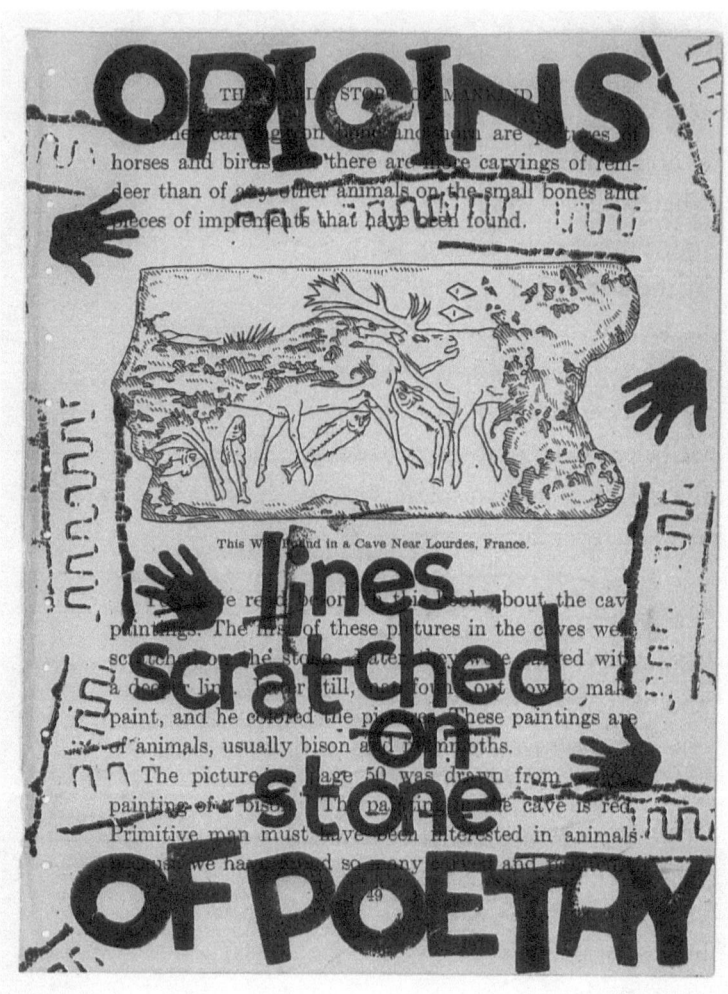

Origins of Poetry: Lines by Joel Lipman

The Players:

Michael Joseph Arcangelini is the author of Waiting for the Wind to Rise, NightBallet Press, 2018.

Jackie Magnuson Ash grew up in Saline County, on a medium-sized farm, surrounded by a family of readers. After a college education, she expected to weave the written word into the fabric of marriage and children. The passing years gave her more than she could have imagined. She's been published in various journals and magazines, including *PlainSpoken: Chosen Lives, Chosen Words, Kansas Voices* (2000-2004) and Caryn Mirriam-Goldberg's *Begin Again*, an anthology of Kansas poets. She currently lives with her husband in Lindsborg.

Jason Baldinger is a poet hailing from Pittsburgh and recently finished a stint as writer in residence at the Osage Arts Community. He's the author of several books, the most recent are *This Useless Beauty* (Alien Buddha Press), *The Ugly Side of the Lake* (Night Ballet Press) written with John Dorsey and the chaplet *Fumbles Revelations* (Grackle and Crow) which are available now. You can hear Jason read poems on recent and forthcoming releases by Theremonster and Sub Pop Recording artist The Gotobeds as well as at jasonbaldinger.bandcamp.com

James Benger is a father, a husband, and writer . His work has been featured in *Coal City Review, Comma Splice, Hoarding Words, Kansas City Voices, Kiosk, Runaway Pony, Thorny Locust*, and *To The Stars Through Difficulties*.

Dianne Borsenik is active in the northern Ohio poetry scene and regional reading circuit, and travels throughout the Midwest to perform her poetry. Her work has been widely published in journals and anthologies, including *Main Street Rag, Chiron Review, Slipstream,* and *Rosebud.* In 2011, she founded NightBallet Press, and has since designed, edited, and published, over one hundred titles for poets across the United States. Lit Youngstown selected her poem *Disco* to print on their tee shirts, which makes her feel like a rock star. Find her on Facebook, and at www.dianneborsenik.com.

Steve Brightman lives in Akron OH with his wife and their parrot. He firmly believes that there are only two seasons: winter and baseball.

Jane McElroy Butler was born in New Jersey and grew up in Ohio. She began writing poetry as a young girl and attended the Young Authors conferences growing up. As an adult, she continued to write but seven years ago lost her sight and became blind. Many of her poems stem from her inner imagination. She has been published in *Khroma* and *Red Fez.*

Xanath Caraza is a traveler, educator, poet and short story writer. She writes for *La Bloga, Smithsonian Latino Center, Seattle Escribe and Revista Literaria Monolito.* For the 2018 International Latino Book Awards, she received First Place for *Lágrima roja* and *Sin preámbulos/Without Preamble* for "Best Book of Poetry in Spanish" and "Best Book Bilingual Poetry". Syllables of Wind received the 2015 International Book Award for Poetry. Her books of verse *Where the Light* is Violet, Black Ink, Ocelocíhuatl, Conjuro and her book of short fiction What the Tide Brings have won national and international recognition. Her other books of poetry are Hudson, Le sillabe del vento, Noche de colibríes, Corazón pintado, and her second short story collection, Metztli. Caraza has been translated into English, Italian, and Greek; and partially translated into Nahuatl, Portuguese, Hindi, Turkish, and Rumanian.

John Clayton is a long-time Maries County, Missouri resident. He lives with his wife, Dawn, on 56 acres where, except for invasive species, and his garden, nature is left to take her course.

Victor Clevenger spends his days in a Madhouse and his nights writing poetry. He lives with his second ex-wife, and together they raise six children in a small town northeast of Kansas City, MO. Selected pieces of his work have appeared in print magazines and journals around the world, as well as at a variety of places online. In 2017, Victor was nominated for the Best of the Net Anthology, as well as the Pushcart Prize. His most recent published collections of poetry include a split book with Tom Farris titled Ginger Roots Are Best Taken Orally (EMP, 2018) and A Finger in the Hornets' Nest (Red Flag Press, 2018).

Daniel Crocker's work has appeared in The Los Angeles Review, Hobart, Big Muddy, New World Writing, Stirring, Juked, The Chiron Review, The Mas Tequila Review and over 100 others. He was the first winner of the Gerald Locklin Prize in poetry. He is the editor of The Cape Rock (Southeast Missouri State University) and the co-editor of Trailer Park Quarterly. He's also the host of the podcast, Sanesplaining, about poetry, mental illness and nerd stuff.

John Dorsey lived for several years in Toledo, Ohio. He is the author of several collections of poetry, including *Teaching the Dead to Sing: The Outlaw's Prayer* (Rose of Sharon Press, 2006), *Sodomy is a City in New Jersey* (American Mettle Books, 2010), *Tombstone Factory* (Epic Rites Press, 2013), *Appalachian Frankenstein* (GTK Press, 2015) *Being the Fire* (Tangerine Press, 2016) and *Shoot the Messenger* (Red Flag Press, 2017). He is the current Poet Laureate of Belle, MO. His work has been nominated for the Pushcart Prize. He may be reached at archerevans@yahoo.com

Greg Edmondson was born in Durham, North Carolina. He earned his BFA from the University of Tennessee, Knoxville and MFA from Washington University in St. Louis. He is the recipient of numerous grants and awards including Fulbright and DAAD fellowships to Germany, and residency fellowships to Artpark, the Virginia Center for the Creative Arts and the Santa Fe Art Institute. He has shown widely throughout the United States and Europe and has works in collections both public and private. Currently Greg is an artist in residence at Osage Arts Community in Belle, Missouri.

Zach Fishel is a graduate of the Pennsylvania coal towns. He's written and taught on three continents and loved them all dearly. At present he resides in the Sonoran Desert hoping friends show up for a quiet dinner or coffee together. He misses trees the most of all.

Michael Hackney holds a BFA from Bowling Green State University's Creative Writing with a specialization in poetry, and a MLS from The University of Toledo with a specialization in teaching English and Writing. My books of poetry and essays can be found at America-Star Books and Chipmunka Publishing, UK. I have received grants and awards from the Toledo Arts Commission and The Ohio Arts Council.

Mark Sebastian Jordan is a freelance writer who lives in the rural central highlands of Ohio. He is known for his trilogy of historical dramas *Ceely, Phoebe,* and *Louie.* He writes for *Seen & Heard International* as a music critic, writes for the arts blog *Voices from the Borderlands,* does a local history column for *Knox Pages,* has two chapbooks of poetry *The Book of Jobs* (Pudding House Press) and *Murder Ballads: American Crime Poems* (Poet's Haven Press), an outrageous mystery *Slammer, Private Dick* (Sinister Hand Media), and a history textbook satire *1776 & All That* (XOXOX Press). In 2018 he was awarded an individual excellence grant from the Ohio Arts Council for his criticism.

Don Kloss is a 60-year-old poet from Central Ohio. His poems have been published twenty-seven times in journals, chapbooks, and online. He has been nominated for Best of the Net. His published collections include *Big Time* and *Gnawing on a Friend.*

Paul Koniecki hosts Pandora's Box Poetry Showcase at Deep Vellum Books in Dallas, Texas. His chapbook, *Reject Convention,* was published by Kleft Jaw Press, 2015 and his poems have appeared in a variety of journals and anthologies since 1985. He was chosen for the Ashbery Home School Residency in Hudson, New York in 2016 . His book, *After Working Hours* was released in July of 2017 by NightBallet Press.

Appointed the first Poet Laureate of Lucas County (2008-2014), by the Board of County Commissioners, **Joel Lipman** was raised in Kenosha, Wisconsin and has lived in Madison, Chicago, Buffalo and Toledo. Awarded Ohio's Governor's Award in 1988 and the 2011 Ohioana State Library's Pegasus Award for Lifetime Achievement, his poems are at https://www.poetryfoundation.org/poets/joel-lipman and currently in Inland Seas: Quarterly Journal of the National Museum of the Great Lakes (V73, Fall 2017, No.3).

John Macker, originally from Colorado, has been an award winning poet and short story writer for over 25 years. His work continues to appear in magazines and anthologies throughout the U.S. and Canada. His latest book is *Disassembled Badlands*. He is also the author of *The Royal Road: Impressions of El Camino Real, Underground Sky, Woman of the Disturbed Earth, Las Montanas de Santa Fe* and *Adventures in the Gun Trade*. His poetry has been nominated for several Pushcart Prizes and in 2006 he won *mad blood magazine's* first annual literary arts award for his long poem, *Wyoming Arcane*.

Chigger Matthews is a language artist living in the American Midwest. Hosts the collaborative feature "Free Chigger Matthews Presents," teaches poetry workshops for all ages, and is an artist-in-residence at Osage Arts Community in Belle, MO. He is the chief editor for *The Artifact, Planet Earth's First Global Poetry Newspaper* and his work appears at home and abroad.

Jason Mayer spent the first part of his adult life as a Marine Corps Combat Correspondent covering stories on five continents and more than 50 countries. After leaving the Marine Corps, he spent eight years working with government contractors supervising the development of more than 200 annual publishing projects. He is the author of *Parables of Lucas Fosterman* and *Fuzzy Dragons & Wild Yetis: A Kid-Friendly Introduction to the Wonderful World of Poetry.* Jason also owns a construction company that designs, builds, and sells playgrounds and recreation projects. He has degrees in Communications and Business Management and an MBA from the University of Maryland. Jason lives in Columbia, Missouri with his wife Angela and two boys, Noah and Caleb.

April Pameticky moved to Wichita in 2002 and somehow finds herself there still. The mother of two shares time between her high school English classroom and the burgeoning creative community of artists and writers in Kansas. She facilitated the Wichita Broadside Project 2017 and currently serves as editor of *River City Poetry,* an online poetry journal and co-edits *Voices of Kansas,* a regional anthology of work from school-aged children across the state. Her own work can be seen in journals like *Malpais Review, KONZA,* and *Chiron Review.* She is also the author of several chapbooks, *Sand River* and *Other Places I've Been* from Finishing Line Press; and *Anatomy of a Sea Star,* from Casa de Cinco Hermanas Press.

R.C. Patterson was born and raised in the City of St. Louis. He has a Masters in Philosophy from the University of Missouri-St. Louis and he teaches philosophy at Harris-Stowe State University. He has self-published several books including *Elegies, Black Lives Splatter,* and *Jim CroMagnon Man.* He is currently working on a novel and a short story collection.

Americana songwriter and Kansas-City-based storyteller **K.W. Peery** is the author of seven poetry collections: *Tales of a Receding Hairline; Purgatory; Wicked Rhythm; Ozark Howler; Gallatin Gallows; Howler Holler; Bootlegger's Bluff.* **Hunter Pender** is a proud Midwestern poet, in 2017 she performed her first featured reading for First Friday in Belle, Missouri.

Jeanette Powers is a poet-artist river-baby non-binary queer and a workaholic: let's build things together. They have blue nails, sand stone and can light a fire without a match, as long as you have a lighter. Also, you have to be friends with the hound dog, Ollymas. They are most recently published by NightBallet Press with *Gasconade,* a founding contributor to FountainVerse: KC Small Press Poetry Fest and Editor in Abetting for Stubborn Mule Press as well as running the performing arts venue Uptown Arts Bar in KCMO. jeanettepowers.com

Karl Ramberg studied piano at Kansas University but dropped out (several times, he says). He volunteered as Elden Tefft's assistant when the Lawrence sculptor was still teaching at KU, learning to carve stone without ever taking a class. He taught himself to compose music by checking out books at the library. Now, the only places in his two-story home not cluttered with instruments, easels, canvases and art supplies are a corner of the kitchen and a tiny upstairs loft with a mattress on the floor.

Dan Smith has a chapbook, *Crooked River,* published by Deep Cleveland Press and another entitled *The Liquid of Her Skin, the Suns of Her Eyes* published by Night

Ballet Press. He likes to rock out with the Deep Cleveland Trio. Check out their CD at CD Baby.

Nathanael Stolte is the author of six chapbooks, most recently *Ramshackle American* (Analogue Submissions Press, 2017). His poems have appeared in various digital and print, anthologies and periodicals. He lives in Buffalo, NY where he is the Acquisitions Editor of CWP Collective Press (www.cwpcollectivepress.com). He is a madcap, flower-punk, corn-fed poet. He replies to emails at nathanaelstolte@yahoo.com.

Kerry Trautman is often seen at local poetry readings and events such as Artomatic 419, 100-Thousand Poets for Change, Back to Jack, and the Columbus Arts Festival. Kerry is a graduate of the University of Toledo Honors College, and is a member of the Ohio Poetry Association. Her poetry and short fiction have appeared in various journals, including *Midwestern Gothic, Alimentum, The American Journal of Nursing, The Coe Review, The Fourth River, Slippery Elm,* and *Third Wednesday;* as well as in anthologies such as, *Tuesday Night at Sam and Andy's Uptown Café* (Westron Press, 2001), *Mourning Sickness* (Omniarts, 2008), *Roll* (Telling Our Stories Press, 2012), and *Journey to Crone* (Chuffed Buff Books, 2013). Kerry has placed several times in the Toledo Museum of Art's annual ekphrastic poetry contest, and she was nominated for a Pushcart Prize in 2017, for her poem *Pixie Cut.* Her chapbooks are, *Things That Come in Boxes* (King Craft Press 2012,) *To Have Hoped* (Finishing Line Press, 2015,) and *Artifacts* (NightBallet Press, 2017).

Agnes Vojta is an Associate Professor of Physics at Missouri University of Science & Technology.

Maryfrances Wagner's books include *Salvatore's Daughter, Light Subtracts Itself, Dioramas, Pouf, Silence of Red Glass, and Red Silk*, winner of the Thorpe Menn Book Award. Poems have appeared in *New Letters, Midwest Quarterly, Laurel Review, Natural Bridge, Voices in Italian Americana, Birmingham Poetry Review, Louisville Review, Poetry East, Unsettling America: An Anthology of Contemporary Multicultural Poetry* (Penguin Books), *Literature Across Cultures* (Pearson/Longman), and *The Dream Book, An Anthology of Writings by Italian American Women* (winner of the American Book Award from the Before Columbus Foundation. Work from that book was chosen for American Audio Prose and was translated into Italian for Trapani Nuovo in Italy). In addition she has published work in many other journals and anthologies. She co-edits the *I-70 Review*, co-edited the *Whirlybird Anthology of Greater Kansas City Writers, Missouri Poets: An Anthology,* and *New Letters Review of Books.* She has served as Co-president of The Writers Place in Kansas City and is active within the writing community. A dog lover, she and her husband, Greg Field, live with Sylvie Plath and Annie Sexton, two dogs they rescued. Maryfrances has taught academic and creative writing as well as mentored, coordinated, and facilitated at all levels. She has lived in the Greater Kansas City area all of her life.

George Wallace is Writer in Residence at the Walt Whitman Birthplace, first poet laureate of Suffolk County, LI NY and author of 33 books and chapbooks of poetry, published in the US, UK, Italy, Macedonia and India. A prominent figure on the NYC poetry performance scene, he travels internationally to perform, lead writing workshops, and lecture on literary topics. A former student of W.D. Snodgrass (BA, Syracuse U) and Marvin Bell (MFA, Pacific U), he teaches writing at Pace University (NYC) and Westchester Community College, and has done research residencies at Harvard's Center for Hellenic Studies in Washington DC. He has worked as a Peace Corps Volunteer, health care administrator, community organizer, community journalist, active duty medical military officer and local historian. His work is collected at the Special Sections Collection, LI Studies Institute, Hofstra University.

John P. Waterman (John P. Waterman) is the author/illustrator of the young adult poetry book, *Such a Little Apple: Anatomoy of a Bully,* the memoir, *Ill Digestions,* and various poetry and photography books. John E. Epic is a performing poet, appearing across 50 stages from Rochester, NY to Topeka, KS. He is also editor and cover designer at *DroneBee Gazette,* a publishing agency for underground writers and artists.

Dan Wright is the in house poet at Dunaway Books in St. Louis and the author of several collections published by Bad Jacket Press.

Scot Young is the editor of *Rusty Truck* and founder of the Rusty Truck Press Brown Bag Chapbook Series.

This project was made possible, in part, by generous support from the Osage Arts Community.

Osage Arts Community provides temporary time, space and support for the creation of new artistic works in a retreat format, serving creative people of all kinds — visual artists, composers, poets, fiction and nonfiction writers. Located on a 152-acre farm in an isolated rural mountainside setting in Central Missouri and bordered by ¾ of a mile of the Gasconade River, OAC provides residencies to those working alone, as well as welcoming collaborative teams, offering living space and workspace in a country environment to emerging and mid-career artists. For more information, visit us at www.osageac.org

www.ingramcontent.com/pod-product-compliance
Lightning Source LLC
Chambersburg PA
CBHW030109100526
44591CB00009B/337